Unconditional Surrender:
The Capture of Forts Henry and Donelson

Civil War Campaigns and Commanders Series

Under the General Editorship of Grady McWhiney

Published

Unconditional Surrender:
The Capture of Forts Henry and Donelson

Spencer C. Tucker

McWhiney Foundation Press
McMurry University
Abilene, Texas

Cataloging-in-Publication Data

Tucker, Spencer, 1937-
      Unconditional surrender: the capture of Forts Henry and
      Donelson / by Spencer C. Tucker.
      p.cm.—(Civil War campaigns and commanders series)
      Includes bibliographical references and index.
      ISBN 1-893114-10-4 (pbk.)

      1. Fort Henry (Tenn.), Battle of, 1862. 2. Fort Donelson
(Tenn.), Battle of, 1862. I. Title. II. Series.

      E472.96 .T83 2001
      973.7'31—dc21

                          2001030384
                                 CIP

McMurry Station, Box 637
Abilene, TX 79697-0637

Printed in the United States of America

ISBN 1-893114-10-4
10 9 8 7 6 5 4 3 2 1

Book Designed by Rosenbohm Graphic Design

All inquiries regarding volume purchases of this book should be
addressed to McWhiney Foundation Press, McMurry Station, Box 637,
Abilene, TX 79697-0637.
Telephone inquiries may be made by calling (915) 793-3862

www.mcwhiney.org

A Note on the Series

Few segments of America's past excite more interest than Civil War battles and leaders. This ongoing series of brief, lively, and authoritative books–*Civil War Campaigns and Commanders*–salutes this passion with inexpensive and accurate accounts that are readable in a sitting. Each volume, separate and complete in itself, nevertheless conveys the agony, glory, death, and wreckage that defined America's greatest tragedy.

In this series, designed for Civil War enthusiasts as well as the newly recruited, emphasis is on telling good stories. Photographs and biographical sketches enhance the narrative of each book, and maps depict events as they happened. Sound history is meshed with the dramatic in a format that is just lengthy enough to inform and yet satisfy.

Grady McWhiney
General Editor

The Publisher Wishes to Dedicate this Volume to
Drake and Mary Bush
Who Brought this Series to Life

CONTENTS

CAMPAIGNS AND COMMANDERS SERIES

Map Key

Geography

 Trees

 Marsh

 Fields

 Strategic Elevations

Rivers

 Tactical Elevations

 Fords

Orchards

— — — — Political Boundaries

Human Construction

 Bridges

 Railroads

 Tactical Towns

 ● ○ Strategic Towns

 □ ■ Buildings

 † Church

 Roads

Military

 Union Infantry

 Confederate Infantry

 Cavalry

Artillery

 Headquarters

Encampments

 Fortifications

 Permanant Works

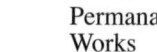 Hasty Works

 Obstructions

 Engagements

 Warships

 Gunboats

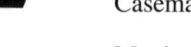 Casemate Ironclad

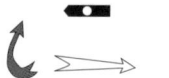 Monitor

 Tactical Movements

 Strategic Movements

Maps by
**Donald S. Frazier, Ph.D.
Abilene, Texas**

MAPS

PHOTOGRAPHS AND ILLUSTRATIONS

Unconditional Surrender:
The Capture of Forts Henry and Donelson

1
SETTING THE STAGE

The 1862 Federal effort to seize Confederate Forts Henry and Donelson in Tennessee, known also as the Twin Rivers Campaign, although early in the conflict, became one of the crucial events of the Civil War. Indeed, the capture of Fort Henry on the Tennessee River on February 6 and that of Fort Donelson on the Cumberland ten days later, gave the Union its first significant victories of the war and opened Tennessee and the Deep South to Federal invasion.

The first major clash of the war, the Battle of Bull Run or Manassas, convinced most observers that the conflict would be neither short nor simple. The United States and the Confederacy got down to the business of war, raising armies and building navies, and looking for the right men to lead them. Americans both North and South rallied to support a war that would eventually touch most every community and every state—even those that hoped to remain neutral.

The conflict spread across three principal theaters of war. The Eastern, the land east of the Appalachian Mountains, was the scene of much fighting—Virginia alone would claim half of all Civil War battles. The Trans-Mississippi, the vast area west of the Mississippi River, drew much less attention. In between lay the Western Theater, which would produce many of the war's most decisive battles. While the East, which embraced the rival capitals, attracted more interest, it was in the Western Theater, many believed, that the war would be won or lost.

The Western Theater encompassed the vast area between the Appalachian Mountains to the east and the Mississippi River to the west, including the seceded states of Alabama, Georgia, Mississippi, and Tennessee, as well as neutral Kentucky. Tennessee, the last state to join the Confederacy, was the key. Its railroads and rivers provided important links to the Deep South and the Trans-Mississippi West. If Union forces could control these avenues, the rest of the South would be dangerously exposed.

The Confederacy could ill afford to lose Tennessee. As a major food-producing state, it was critical to survival of Confederate armies in the field. Its capital, Nashville, was a major rail center and one of the most important arms manufacturing centers in the Confederacy, producing cannon, small arms, percussion caps, cartridges, and sabers. Nashville facilities also turned out uniforms and leather goods. Along the Cumberland River northwest of Nashville lay the South's largest gunpowder mills. The state also held two-thirds of the Confederacy's mineral wealth. This included one of the South's largest iron-producing regions, located between the Tennessee and Cumberland rivers, and ninety percent of its copper.

At the beginning of the war few leaders North or South sensed the full importance of Tennessee; there were no precise military plans for taking or defending the state. Federal General-in-Chief Winfield Scott's "Anaconda Plan" called for

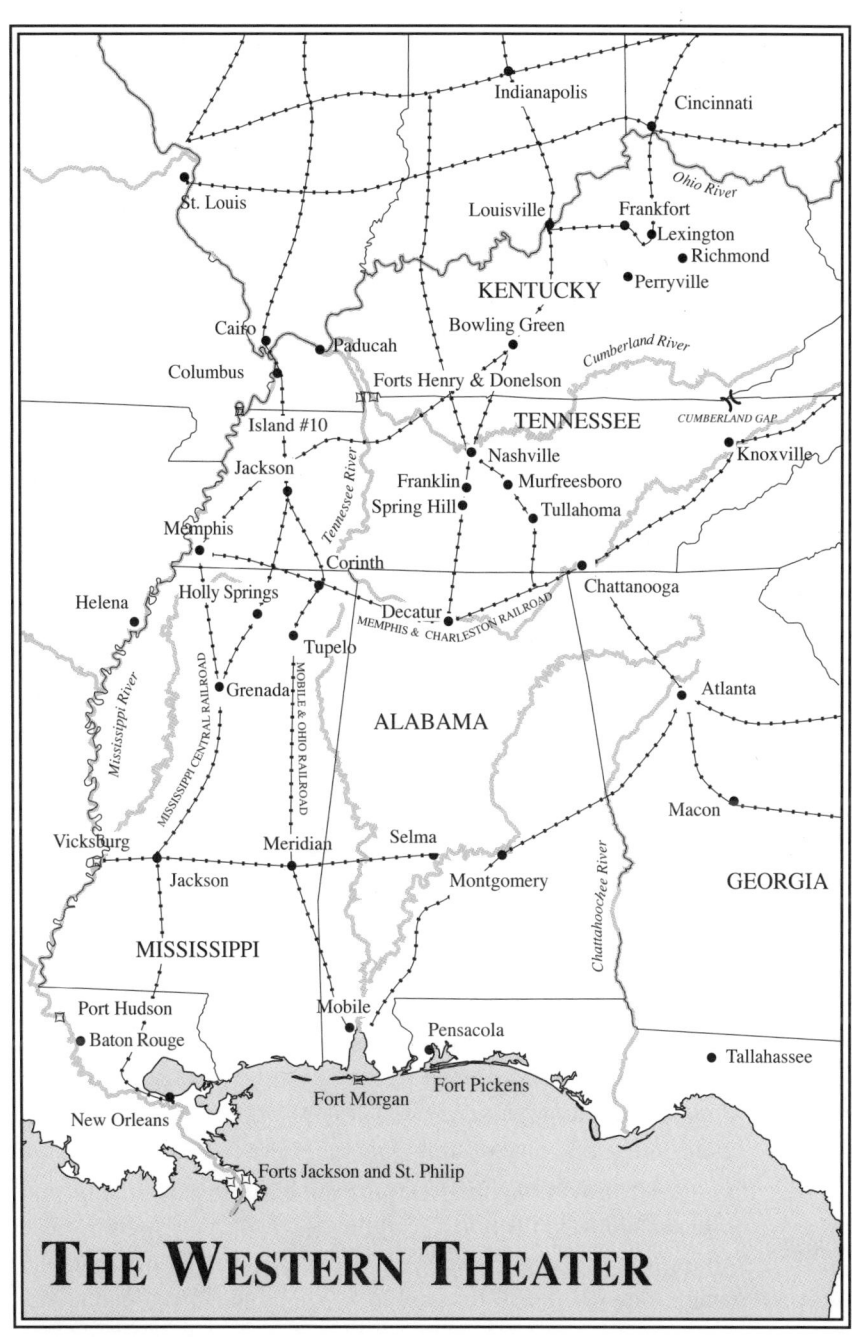

THE WESTERN THEATER

splitting the Confederacy along the Mississippi River and strangling it with a naval blockade of its ports. President Abraham Lincoln wanted an invasion—-bold simultaneous attacks from Cairo, Illinois, against Memphis and from Cincinnati, Ohio, into East Tennessee, an area of strong Union sympathy. This idea ignored central Tennessee in favor of the Mississippi. Major General George B. McClellan proposed to send 80,000 troops against Nashville in conjunction with an Atlantic coast pincer movement from Charleston toward Augusta, Georgia. Later he proposed operations to secure Missouri, a thrust down the Mississippi, and operations in Eastern Tennessee to seize railroads from Memphis to the East.

McClellan well understood the importance of railroads in moving troops and supplies. Securing Southern railroads could paralyze the Confederate army and win the war for the North. He came to favor a plan by which several Federal armies would move southward from Ohio along different routes, reunite at Chattanooga, and then march on Atlanta in conjunction with expeditions against Charleston and New Orleans.

The first major Union foray in the Western Theater came in October 1861, when Brigadier General William "Bull" Nelson carried out what amounted to little more than a raid into eastern Kentucky. Brigadier General William T. Sherman, then commanding the Department of the Cumberland, did not encourage a thrust into Tennessee. He informed McClellan that his available force was "too small to do good and too large to sacrifice." Confederate defenses were reportedly well developed, and the lack of good roads and adequate rail lines presented serious difficulties.

In early November, with Missouri largely secure, Lincoln reorganized the Western Department. After consulting with new General-in-Chief McClellan, he replaced incompetent commander Major General John C. Frémont and installed Major General Henry Halleck as commander of the newly designated Department of the Missouri, which embraced Missouri, Iowa, Minnesota, Illinois, Arkansas, and Kentucky west of the Cumberland River. Also, Brigadier General Don Carlos Buell assumed command of the Department of the Ohio, which included Ohio, Michigan, Indiana, and the portion of Kentucky east of the Cumberland River. The dividing line between the two departments was drawn so as to give Buell, considered one of the best generals in the Union Army (with a command that McClellan considered second only to his own), access to the Cumberland River for a thrust against Nashville. Federal armies were not confined to the geographical boundaries of their various departments. Lincoln now pressed his new commanders—McClellan, Buell, and Halleck—to get on with the task at hand.

At the beginning of 1862 Union forces in the West outnumbered the Confederates two to one. Halleck at St. Louis had 30,000 men. His subordinate, thirty-nine-year-old Brigadier General Ulysses S. Grant, commanded the District of Cairo, at the southern tip of Illinois, with 20,000 men at his disposal. Among these were forces at the mouths of the Tennessee and Cumberland rivers under sixty-year-old Brigadier General Charles F. Smith. Regarded as one of the best soldiers in the Union Army, Smith had been Grant's instructor at West Point and was three times breveted for bravery during the Mexican War. Buell, commander of the Department of the Ohio with headquarters at Louisville, commanded 70,000 men posted at various spots within the department (of whom perhaps 57,000 were effectives).

Both Buell and Halleck, citing logistical problems and insufficient resources, delayed offensive action as they bickered back and forth and communicated frequently with McClellan. Lincoln wanted concurrent attacks to put maximum pressure on Confederate defenses, but his two commanders in the West each sought priority for his own plans. Buell wanted to attack Bowling Green, but only if supported by Halleck;

Halleck favored a thrust up the Tennessee River, but only if Buell was in a supporting role. Each, anxious to outdo the other, feared risking failure. Dividing the Union command in the Western theater had been a serious mistake.

The Confederates, on the other hand, possessed unity of command. General Albert Sidney Johnston had charge of the Confederate Western Military Department. Although he had never commanded a major army in the field, many people on both sides of the conflict considered him America's ablest officer. Born in Kentucky in 1803 and educated at Transylvania University, he was a close friend of fellow Transylvania alum-

HENRY W. HALLECK

Born New York 1815; Halleck was graduated from the U.S. Military Academy in 1839, third in his class of thirty-one; commissioned a 2d lieutenant of engineers, he worked on New York Harbor's fortifications and made an inspection tour of France; promoted to 1st lieutenant, he served in California during the Mexican War, earning a brevet to captain; an astute military thinker, "Old Brains," as he was called, authored *Report on the Means of National Defense* and *Elements of Military Art and Science*; he also translated Henri Jomini's *Vie Politique et Militaire de Napoleon*; promoted to the full rank of captain in 1853, Halleck resigned his commission the following year; he entered a lucrative legal practice in San Francisco, wrote two volumes on mining law, helped draft California's constitution, and was active in the state militia; with the onset of the Civil War, General Winfield Scott recommended Halleck to President Abraham Lincoln; commissioned directly into the regular army as a major general, Halleck became the fourth ranking officer in the army, following Scott, George B. McClellan, and John C. Frémont; always an effective administrator, Halleck took command of the Department of the

nus Confederate President Jefferson Davis. Johnston had graduated from West Point in 1826 two years ahead of Davis and served creditably in the Black Hawk War. He was a brigadier general in the army of the Republic of Texas and its secretary of war from 1838 to 1840. In the Mexican War he commanded a volunteer regiment but saw little fighting. He rejoined the regular army in 1849 as a paymaster, but in 1855 then Secretary of War Davis appointed Johnston colonel of the newly formed 2nd United States Cavalry, an elite regiment that included many future Civil War generals among its officers. Johnston led the 1857-1858 expedition against the Mormons

Missouri in November 1861, succeeding Frémont, and brought much-needed order to the chaotic West; in March his command was extended and redesignated the Department of the Mississippi; much of his department's success came with the battlefield accomplishments of his subordinates, Generals U.S. Grant (Forts Henry and Donelson, Shiloh), Samuel Curtis (Pea Ridge), and John Pope (Island No. 10); Halleck, however, proved an inept field commander when, after Shiloh, he took control of Grant's army and failed to crush the badly outnumbered Rebels at Corinth; named commander in chief of U.S. forces, Halleck moved to Washington, D.C., where his role became increasingly advisory and administrative; displaced by Grant's promotion in March 1864, Halleck became chief of staff and served credibly for the balance of the war; afterward, he headed the Military Division of the James, from April to June 1865, and the Division of the Pacific until 1869, when he assumed command of the Division of the South, headquartered at Louisville, Kentucky; he died there in 1872. General Halleck was extremely unpopular among his fellow officers and members of the Lincoln Administration; he owned a poor disposition, was difficult to work with, and frequently criticized other generals; this, combined with poor leadership qualities and his demonstrated inability as a field commander, left him the target of much ridicule; but he was a fine administrator and as such contributed greatly to the Federal victory and was especially useful after Grant became commanding general.

in Utah, and at the outbreak of the war he was a brevet brigadier general in command of the Department of the Pacific. He declined a high command in the Union army and resigned his commission upon the secession of his adopted state of Texas. Davis, now the Confederate president, proclaimed Johnston "the greatest soldier, the ablest man, civil or military, Confederate or Federal," and appointed him a full general, ranking him second on the army list only to Adjutant

ALBERT SIDNEY JOHNSTON

Born Kentucky 1803; after attending Transylvania University, he entered the U.S. Military Academy in 1822, graduating eighth in his 1826 class of forty-one; breveted 2d lieutenant and posted to infantry, he served on the frontier and in the 1832 Black Hawk War; in 1834 he resigned his commission to care for his dying wife; after her death he moved to revolutionist Texas; in 1837 he became senior brigadier in the new republic's army and served two years as secretary of war; during the war with Mexico, Johnston commanded a regiment of Texas volunteers and saw action at Monterrey; he reentered the U.S. Army in 1849 as a major and paymaster to the military posts in Texas; in 1855 he was promoted to colonel and given command of the new 2d Cavalry, an elite regiment that included among its officers such future Civil War generals as Robert E. Lee, George Thomas, William J. Hardee, and John Bell Hood; shortly thereafter he also assumed command of the Department of Texas; in 1857 Johnston headed an expedition to Utah to quell Mormon unrest, a difficult assignment that garnered him a brevet promotion to brigadier general; he then assumed command of the Department of the Pacific with headquarters at San Francisco, and was on duty there when his adopted home state Texas seceded from the Union; resigning his U.S. commission a second time,

General Samuel Cooper. In September 1861 Davis gave Johnston what was certainly one of the most daunting assignments of the war—-command of the broad, river-threaded Western Theater (or Confederate Department Number Two). It fell to Johnston to defend the Southern heartland against vastly superior Federal land and naval forces.

The Confederates had hoped to fix their northern frontier on the Ohio River, but Kentucky's proclamation of neutrality

Johnston traveled overland from California to Virginia to offer his services to the Confederacy, arriving at Richmond in August 1861; considered by many America's foremost military man, he was received warmly by his friend and fellow West Point cadet, Confederate President Jefferson Davis, who appointed him full general (ranking second only to Adjutant General Samuel Cooper in the Confederate army); given command of the Western Theater (Department No. 2), Johnston worked to hold the vast region, but the surrenders of Forts Henry and Donelson in February 1862 opened Tennessee to Federal invasion and forced a general retreat southward; after concentrating his forces at Corinth, Mississippi, Johnston in early April 1862 attacked General U.S. Grant's Federal army near Pittsburg Landing, on the Tennessee River in southwestern Tennessee; the attack surprised the Federals and promised great success, but at the height of the fighting Johnston fell wounded and bled to death on the field; General P.G.T. Beauregard suspended the attack late in the day; the next day reenforced Federal troops drove the Confederates from the field; the Battle of Shiloh was the first great contest of the war and one of the bloodiest in U.S. history. Johnston had received much criticism for the loss of Tennessee, but Davis stood by his friend. A major controversy, fueled by Beauregard and his supporters on one side and William Preston Johnston (his son) on the other, developed over Johnston's role at Shiloh and the quality of his generalship. Johnston's death early in the battle and so early in the war make an evaluation of his overall generalship impossible. Although he certainly lost more ground than he won during his brief Civil War career, at the time of his death he appeared to be on the verge of a stunning victory. General Johnston's remains were eventually removed to the Texas State Cemetery in Austin.

precluded this. Kentucky did, however provide a shield for the defense of Tennessee, a political barrier to Federal invasion, which the Confederates now proceeded to undo.

On September 4, before Johnston's arrival, Confederate Major General and Episcopal bishop Leonidas Polk committed one of the major blunders of the Civil War. He ordered Brigadier General Gideon J. Pillow to fortify Columbus, Kentucky, on the Mississippi River twenty miles below Cairo. This violation of Kentucky's neutrality gave the Union an excuse to intervene in the state. Two days after the Confederates seized Columbus, General Grant, acting on his own initiative, took Paducah, an important Ohio River town forty-five miles from Cairo at the confluence of the Tennessee and Ohio Rivers. Grant then positioned troops at Smithfield at the mouth of the Cumberland.

Both sides quickly established positions across the pivotal border state.

The Confederate defense of Tennessee now rested on a line centered on the Tennessee and Cumberland Rivers with the two flanks in advance of the center. The Confederates were operating on the outside of the arc, or exterior lines, while Union forces enjoyed the advantage of interior lines. The Confederates' awkward defensive position was partially offset by their control of the railroad from Bowling Green, Kentucky, west to Columbus.

Johnston regarded Columbus as the key to the Western Theater and vowed to construct there a "Gibraltar of the West." Polk soon placed guns on the high bluffs overlooking the river some twenty miles in either direction. By the end of October Polk had 10,000 troops at Columbus and ultimately a large number of guns.

Columbus became the most important Confederate fortification on the great river. The ever-cautious Halleck wrote McClellan on January 20, "Columbus cannot be taken without an immense siege train and a terrible loss of life. I have thor-

LEONIDAS POLK

Born North Carolina 1806; attended the University of North Carolina and then the U.S. Military Academy, graduating eighth in his class of thirty-eight in 1827; brevetted 2d lieutenant and posted to artillery, Polk served only a few months before resigning to study for the Episcopal ministry; ordained a deacon in 1830, he became Missionary Bishop of the Southwest in 1838 and Bishop of Louisiana in 1841; assisted in the establishment of the University of the South at Sewanee, Tennessee; at the outbreak of the Civil War, Polk accepted a major general's commission from his close friend Confederate President Jefferson Davis; Polk's departmental command consisted of parts of Arkansas and western Tennessee. In September 1861 he violated Kentucky's professed neutrality by occupying Columbus, opening that state to Federal invasion; commanded a corps with gallantry but little skill at Shiloh and in the invasion of Kentucky; promoted to lieutenant general in October 1862, he directed a corps at Murfreesboro and a wing at Chickamauga; his overt criticism of General Braxton Bragg resulted in his banishment from the Army of Tennessee; he was given command of the Department of Alabama, Mississippi, and East Louisiana where he remained until ordered, in May 1864, to join  the Army of Tennessee, now headed by Bragg's replacement General J.E. Johnston; Polk led his army (in effect, a corps) during the opening stages of the Atlanta Campaign; on June 14, 1864 he was instantly killed when struck by a solid shot while surveying Federal positions from Pine Mountain near Marietta, Georgia. General Polk's impact on the Confederate cause was largely negative. His violation of Kentucky neutrality proved irreparable and his feud with Bragg severely damaged the effectiveness of the Army of Tennessee. Davis's reluctance to remove Polk only exacerbated the situation.

oughly studied its defenses—they are very strong." But Columbus could be outflanked. As Halleck noted, "it can be turned, paralyzed, and forced to surrender."

Columbus lies reasonably close to where the Tennessee and Cumberland rivers flow into the Ohio. The 650-mile-long Tennessee River rises in eastern Tennessee a few miles above Knoxville, flows through northern Alabama and a corner of Mississippi, returns to Tennessee, and then flows north into Kentucky west of Bowling Green to join the Ohio at Paducah. The circuitous 700-mile-long Cumberland River rises in eastern Kentucky, dips into Tennessee, running through Nashville, and joins the Ohio at Smithland, a few miles above Paducah. Beginning in northern Tennessee, northwest of Nashville, the two rivers run roughly parallel as they flow northward toward the Ohio.

Just south of the Kentucky border, where the Tennessee and Cumberland rivers close to within a dozen miles of each other, the Confederates built two forts: Henry on the east bank of the Tennessee River and Donelson on the western bank of the Cumberland. Actually, the forts were considerably closer together as lines of rifle pits narrowed the gap by several miles. The two forts anchored the middle of the thin Confederate defensive line that ran east from Arkansas, across the Mississippi at Columbus, through Bowling Green (where Johnston established his headquarters) and Mill Springs, and terminated in eastern Kentucky near Cumberland Gap.

Johnston intended the two forts to block any movement by Union forces upriver into central Tennessee and beyond. The forts also protected vital Confederate railroad lines, especially the long route that linked Memphis on the Mississippi to Bowling Green with spurs to Nashville and Chattanooga in Tennessee; Corinth, Mississippi; and Decatur, Alabama. And they guarded the extensive Cumberland Valley iron works. If Henry were taken, Union forces could move by water as far south as Muscle Shoals, Alabama. Were Donelson to fall,

Nashville, seventy miles upriver, would be lost. Should Union forces take both forts they could isolate the Confederate flanks at Bowling Green and Columbus and destroy Johnston's forces piecemeal.

In early 1862 Johnston commanded some 67,500 irregularly armed troops stretched thin along this 500-mile defensive line. At Bowling Green Johnston had 14,000 men, with another 11,000 at various points to southwest. These troops were to block the route south along the Louisville to Nashville railroad. In the center of his line, at Forts Henry and Donelson, were 5,500 men. On the left at Columbus blocking the Mississippi invasion route, Polk commanded 17,000 men. West of the Mississippi in Arkansas, also under Johnston's command, Major General Earl Van Dorn led another 20,000 men.

General Johnston's broad-front defensive line represented a calculated risk, an attempt to convince the Federals that he had at his disposal a much larger force than was the case. He hoped to hold this weak forward line until he could bring up sufficient reinforcements. For some six months this strategy worked well. Indeed, Johnston ordered aggressive small actions that seemed to portend a Confederate invasion of the North, all the time being acutely aware of his own weakness. As early as September 1861 he wrote President Jefferson Davis in Richmond, "We have not over half the armed forces that are now likely to be required for our security against disaster." And the location of Forts Henry and Donelson beckoned just that. There was no natural defensive position south of the two forts. If they fell to the Federals, Johnston would either have to retreat from Kentucky and northern Tennessee or run the risk of having his supply lines severed and his entire army isolated.

General Pierre Gustave Toutant Beauregard, banished by Davis to the West to serve as Johnston's second in command, joined him on February 4, 1862. The Creole was appalled by Johnston's dispositions and told him that he could see no point

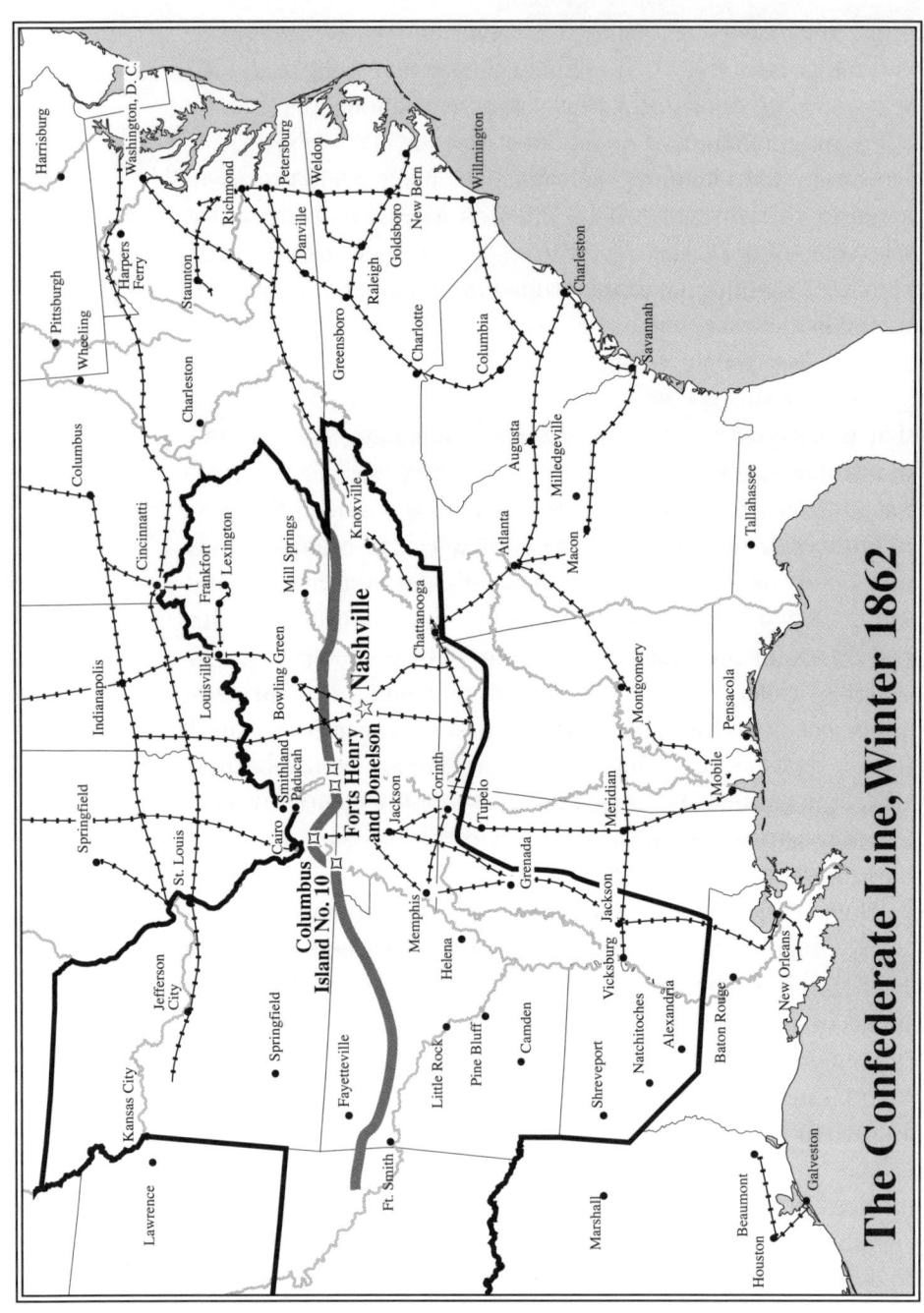

The Confederate Line, Winter 1862

in holding Bowling Green, which would have to be vacated on any Union advance. He advocated abandoning that place and concentrating troops near Henry and Donelson.

Union commanders in the West, meanwhile, were driving Lincoln to distraction by their inaction. While Buell procrastinated in carrying out proposed drives on Bowling Green and Knoxville, Halleck also failed to move. He was busy trying to stabilize Missouri and reorganizing his command.

Halleck, clearly one of the army's brightest officers, proved to be a dismal field commander. A graduate of Union College and West Point (1839) who had traveled to France to study that nation's army, Halleck was both a military theorist and, unlike his rival Grant, a success in civilian life. An expert on fortifications, in 1846 he published as a lieutenant, *Elements of Military Art and Science*, the first American examination of new European military theory. He also translated Swiss writer Antoine Henri Jomini's study of Napoleon. Such pursuits led colleagues to call Halleck "Old Brains."

Like Grant, Halleck resigned his captaincy in the army in 1854, but he settled in California to become successful as a lawyer and businessman and to write two books on law. Halleck reentered the army in August 1861, accepting a commission as a major general. In November he assumed command of the Department of the Missouri.

Halleck, headquartered in St. Louis, was far removed from the Kentucky front. This, combined with his need to restore order in his department after the chaotic management of his predecessor, the threat of a Confederate invasion of Missouri, his jealousy of Buell, and his own cautious tendencies produced inaction. On December 19, 1861, Halleck wrote McClellan:

I am progressing slowly with the reorganization of the forces here. It is a most difficult task, increased by the injudicious orders of the War Department and the jealousies of the Governors of States. The administration and machinery for the supply of the army is rapidly getting into working order. This is a matter of the greatest necessity, and consequently has absorbed most of my attention.

ULYSSES S. GRANT

Born Ohio 1822; graduated U.S. Military Academy 1843, twenty-first in his class; brevetted 2d lieutenant in 4th Infantry 1843; 2d lieutenant 1845; 1st lieutenant 1847; regimental quartermaster 1847 to 1853; brevetted captain 1847 for gallant conduct in Mexican War; assigned in 1852 to duty in California, where he missed his wife and drank heavily; resigned from army in 1854 to avoid court martial; failed at a number of undertakings; appointed colonel 21st Illinois Infantry and then brigadier general volunteers in 1861; major general volunteers 1862; gained national attention following victories at Fort Donelson, Shiloh, and Vicksburg; received thanks of Congress and promotion to major general U.S. Army in 1863; after victories around Chattanooga, appointed lieutenant general and commander of all U.S. forces in 1864. Accompanied Meade's Army of the Potomac on a bloody campaign of attrition through the Wilderness, Spotsylvania, Cold Harbor, siege of Petersburg, and the pursuit to Appomattox; commander of the U.S. Army 1864 to 1869; U.S. president 1869 to 1877. Visited Europe, suffered bankruptcy, and wrote his memoirs while dying of cancer; died in 1885 in New York City, where he is buried. "The art of war is simple enough," Grant once explained. "Find out where your enemy is. Get at him as soon as you can. Strike at him as hard as you can, and keep moving on." A staff officer said of Grant: "His face has three expressions: deep thought, extreme determination, and great simplicity and calmness."

When President Abraham Lincoln prodded him, Halleck replied on January 1, 1862, "Too much haste will ruin everything." Halleck's subordinate, General Grant, needed no such urging.

Hiram Ulysses Grant was born in Point Pleasant, Ohio, in 1822, the son of an ambitious tanner. An error on his Congressional appointment to the U.S. Military Academy caused him to be listed Ulysses Simpson Grant. As it turned out it was a fortunate error, and he let stand his new name of U. S. Grant. He graduated from West Point in the middle of his class in 1843 and served with distinction in the Mexican War, winning brevets for gallantry at Molino del Rey and Chapultepec. After the war he served at a variety of posts, including remote Fort Humbolt in California, but without his wife Julia and their children he took to drink. As a friend put it, "whenever he was idle and depressed, this appetite came upon him." Under censure by his regimental commander, in July 1854 Grant resigned his commission and returned to his home in Missouri. He tried various civilian pursuits, including farming and real estate sales, without success before finally clerking in his father's Galena, Illinois, leather-goods store.

The Civil War gave Grant a second chance. With the outbreak of hostilities he offered his services to the Union and secured the colonelcy of an Illinois regiment. The backing of Congressman Elihu Washburne and early success fighting in Missouri won him promotion to brigadier general in August 1861.

Grant was a man of high intelligence, a gifted organizer and administrator, and an aggressive commander. Unlike many other Civil War generals, he rarely complained, and did his job in a calm, soft-spoken, and professional manner. He cared little for military formalities and was often plain, even negligent, in dress. As writer Shelby Foote noted, "There was an unbuttoned informality about him and about the way he did things; but it involved a good deal more of reticence than congeniality, as if his trust and understanding stopped at horses."

Before his departure as commander of the Western Department, Frémont performed at least one important service for the Union: he picked Grant to command the troops assembling at Cairo, Illinois. On September 4, 1861, Grant arrived at Cairo and took up command of the Southeast Missouri Military District, embracing southern Illinois and southeastern Missouri. Two days after his arrival at Cairo, Grant took the gunboats *Tyler* and *Conestoga* and three steamers to lift 2,000 men and seized Paducah. Riverine warfare had come into its own.

2
RIVERINE WARFARE

Control of the West's great rivers, the Mississippi, the Ohio, the Tennessee, and the Cumberland, was vital to both sides in the war. Unlike those in the East, which tended to obstruct north-to-south troop movements, the big rivers of the West offered splendid avenues of invasion. They also formed immensely important lines of communication in a region of insufficient railroads and very poor roads. Food and war materials could be shipped by water, and it was often considerably quicker to move troops by transport ship than by overland march. The Union relied on this vast river system to bring men, food, and supplies from the East and Midwest to staging areas such as Louisville and Cairo in preparation for a thrust into the Confederacy.

The Western rivers were for the most part shallow and winding, precluding the use of sailing vessels with their traditional broadside batteries. Both Northern and Southern navies needed new vessels, river gunboats: broad-beam, shallow-draft vessels, mounting as many as four guns forward and two aft and others in broadsides. Although the Confederates also built them, the North's superior manufacturing resources allowed it to get gunboats onto the Western waters first.

As early as April 29, 1861, James B. Eads of St. Louis wrote Secretary of the Navy Gideon Welles, suggesting that Cairo, Illinois, where the Ohio and Mississippi Rivers meet, be made the main base for Union gunboat operations. The city offered direct access to the river traffic of Illinois, Kentucky, and Missouri. Eads had been a salvage operator before the war and was quite familiar with operations on the Mississippi. He proposed the conversion of powerful steamers that had been used to pull snags from the river into makeshift gunboats. These "snagboats" would become floating batteries, protected against enemy fire by bales of cotton.

Welles passed Eads' suggestion along to then commander of the Department of the Ohio General McClellan and ordered Navy Commander John Rodgers to Cincinnati to work with McClellan. By June 8, 1861 Rodgers had negotiated contracts to buy and convert three wooden side-wheel steamers into navy gunboats that would, however, be under army control. These were the *Tyler* (ex *A.O. Tyler*), the *Lexington*, and the *Conestoga*. They were strengthened to enable them to carry heavy guns, and 5-inch thick oak siding was installed to act as protection against rifle fire. These "timberclads" were converted at Louisville and were ready for service in late July, although low water prevented their arrival at Cairo until August. On commissioning, the *Conestoga* mounted four 32-pounder smoothbore cannon; the *Lexington* had two 32-pounders and four 64-pounder (8-inch shell) smoothbores. The *Tyler* had six 64-pounder (8-inch shell) guns in broadside batteries and one 32-pounder in the stern.

Eads also traveled to Washington to push for new gunboat construction. In July 1861 Army Quartermaster General

The "timberclad" Conestoga, 1862

Montgomery C. Meigs contracted with Eads to build seven ironclad gunboats for the Army. (These warships were not formally transferred to the Navy until October 1, 1862.)

Designed by John Lenthall, the gunboats were modified by Samuel Pook and Eads. These Cairo- or City-class river ironclads, all named for towns on the Mississippi and Ohio rivers, were also known as "Pook Turtles" because of the rectangular casemates with sloped, armored sides that covered the ships. The seven new ironclads were the *Cairo, Carondelet, Cincinnati, Louisville, Mound City, Pittsburg,* and *St. Louis* (renamed the *Baron de Kalb* when it was transferred to the Navy as there was already a St. Louis in naval service). The 512-ton vessels were 175 feet long, 51.5 feet in beam, and drew only six feet of water. Propelled by a stern paddle wheel located amidships, they were designed to make 9 miles-per-hour but often had trouble reaching that speed when steaming against the current. Their normal crew complement was 251 men.

The gunboats were heavily armed. In January 1862 each mounted thirteen guns: three 8-inch smoothbores, four Army 42-pounder coast defense rifled guns (7-inch bore), and six 32-pounder rifled guns. Each, except the *Pittsburg,* also carried one light 12-pounder Dahlgren boat howitzer, not counted in their ratings. And each gunboat was protected with 2.5

The Federal gunboat *St. Louis*, 1862. One of seven ships of similar design (the Cairo- or City-class river ironclad) named for cities along the Ohio and Mississippi rivers, it later was renamed the *Baron de Kalb*.

inches of armor on the casemate and 1.25 inches on the conical pilothouse forward.

Soon after the contract was signed 4,000 men went to work around the clock, pushing the gunboats to completion. The *Carondelet* was the first gunboat launched, on October 12, 1861, but all were commissioned in January 1862. In a remarkably short time Eads had constructed a squadron of ironclad gunboats that the Union might use in its effort to control Western waters.

Eads later converted two civilian snagboats to ironclads: the *Benton* of 633 tons and the *New Era*, which became the *Essex*, of 355 tons.

Before Eads had his gunboats ready, Navy officials ordered an important command change in the West. John Rodgers' abrasive character and failure to keep Washington informed led to his recall. Secretary Welles selected Captain Andrew Foote, a more senior officer, as Rodgers' replacement. Rodgers complained bitterly to Welles that "when the plant thus watered and cultivated gives its first prematurely ripe fruit, the crop is turned over to another with cold words."

Born at New Haven, Connecticut, in 1806, the son of a future U.S. senator, Foote attended private school with Gideon Welles. Their friendship played an important part in Foote's subsequent career. Foote went to West Point but he stayed there less than a year. He had always been interested in the sea and in 1822 he secured an appointment as a naval midshipman. His first cruise was in the schooner *Grampus*, engaged in suppressing West Indian piracy. A succession of other assignments followed, including an 1839 around-the-world cruise in the sloop of war *John Adams*.

While on a cruise in the *Natchez*, Foote had a religious experience that shaped the rest of his life. His Christian convictions manifested themselves in his strong opposition to slavery and the slave trade and his crusade within the Navy for temperance, which became reality in 1862 with the abolition of the grog ration aboard ships.

Foote failed to get into the Mexican War, but from 1856 to 1858 he did experience a good deal of fighting in China, when he commanded the *Portsmouth* and two other vessels. The United Kingdom and China were then at war, and Foote's task was to keep the United States out of the fighting and at the same time protect American interests. Nonetheless, while Foote was withdrawing his ships from Whampoa, guns in the Chinese Barrier Forts opened fire. With no apology or satisfaction forthcoming, Foote led ashore a party of sailors and Marines and destroyed the forts, then mounting 176 guns. This produced forty U.S. casualties but cost the Chinese several hundred, and Washington subsequently approved Foote's actions.

At the outbreak of the Civil War Foote commanded the New York Navy Yard. In June 1861 he was promoted to captain. On September 12, having been named commander of Union naval forces on the upper Mississippi, Foote arrived at St. Louis.

Welles' had made a wise choice. One of his officers said of Foote that "He could preach, fight or pray with equal facility."

Indeed Foote often preached to his crews on Sunday. He had a blunt manner and implacable resolve and, like Grant, he believed the way to defeat the enemy was to attack him. Brave and determined in battle, he was also a brilliant organizer who got on well with his fellow officers. Certainly, much of the Mississippi River Squadron's success was attributable to his efforts.

Foote faced daunting problems in readying his squadron. He wrote Assistant Secretary of the Navy Gustavus V. Fox, "I only wish that you could have spent one day here for the last six weeks, as no imagination can fancy what it is to collect materials and fit out western gunboats with western men without a navy yard, in the west, where no stores are to be had."

Foote soon established a depot at Cairo for repair and

ANDREW HULL FOOTE

Born at New Haven, Connecticut, in 1806, the son of future U.S. Senator Samuel Foot (Andrew Foote added the "e" to the family name), Foote briefly attended the U.S. Military Academy in 1822, but resigned to become an acting midshipman in the Navy; he served in the West Indies and the Pacific and during a subsequent Caribbean cruise in 1827 he had a religious experience that prompted a lively interest in Christianity and reform; after a cruise around the world from 1837 to 1841 he served as executive officer of the Philadelphia Naval Asylum; in 1843, as first lieutenant, his reform efforts aboard the *Cumberland* made it the first temperance ship in the Navy; (his continued advocacy of temperance contributed in no small measure to the abolition of spirit ration in the Navy, which occurred in 1862;) from 1849 to 1852 Foote commanded the brig *Perry* in the suppression of the slave trade off the west coast of Africa, after which he produced a book, *Africa and the American Flag*, that called for a greater commitment to the persecution of the slave trade; over the next several years, Foote remained ashore involved in naval reform, including a stint on the efficiency

replenishment of his Mississippi Squadron. Initially, the entire facility was afloat, but later he ordered the construction of a 10-acre navy yard at Mound City just above Cairo, although its machine shops and carpenter shops remained afloat in steamers.

Frémont had signed contracts for the first seven gunboats, then two more, plus thirty-eight mortar boats, each mounting a 13-inch mortar, and several other vessels. All were being built at once with attendant delays. Since no one had any experience building ironclads, there were extensive problems and cost overruns. Finally Meigs informed Foote that the War Department would pay only for the seven gunboats originally authorized. It took McClellan's intervention in December to rectify the situation.

Foote's most difficult challenge was to secure trained crews

board; returning to sea as commander of the sloop *Portsmouth*, in 1856 Foote led a landing party that destroyed four forts guarding the approaches to Canton in retaliation for the Chinese firing on U.S. ships; in command of the Brooklyn Navy Yard at the outbreak of the Civil War, Foote was selected to head the flotilla of gunboats then under construction for service on the Western rivers; he supervised the final preparations and secured crews for the new ironclad warships that he would lead against Confederate fortifications; working in conjunction with the land forces of General U.S. Grant, with whom he formed an excellent partnership, now Flag Officer Foote led his gunboats against Fort Henry on the Tennessee River; on February 6, 1862 Foote's gunboats captured Fort Henry before the army arrived; eight days later Foote's flotilla was turned back at Fort Donelson, which later fell to Grant; slightly wounded in the fierce exchange at Donelson, Foote remained on duty; his gunboats, supported by mortar boats, participated in the subsequent captures of Island Number Ten and Fort Pillow in the Mississippi; but his leg wound that refused to heal, coupled with the strain of relentless campaigning, forced Foote to accept a leave of absence in May 1862; promoted to rear admiral in June, he assumed administrative duties in Washington; in 1863 he was selected to take over the South Atlantic Blockading Squadron off Charleston, but before he could take command he was stricken with Bright's disease. Admiral Foote died at New York City in June 1863. A gifted organizer and bold fighter, Foote set new standards for the conduct of riverine warfare and made an important contribution to the Federal conquest of the South.

for his new weapons. His appeals to the Navy Department brought some men; he sent agents to the Great Lakes to recruit seamen there; some foreigners, mostly Irish, enlisted; and he even called on the War Department. At the end of January 1862 Foote was still short 1,000 men for the gunboats and another 700 for the mortar boats. The War Department authorized Halleck to release qualified men from the Army, but this presented problems. Finally, after ordering operations against Fort Henry, Halleck allowed Grant to detail soldiers for gunboat duty. Other administrative concerns, such as getting his men paid and fed, added to Foote's burden.

It was difficult for Foote or any Navy officer to take orders from the Army. Army officers, even those junior to him, constantly obstructed Foote's commands. An earlier appeal to Frémont brought some results. The general placed under Foote's command all craft and shipping "belonging to the entire floated expedition down the Mississippi River," adding, "and you will also consider yourself in charge of, and commanding this expedition." Also, Welles granted Foote's request that he be given flag rank, the equivalent of major general in the Army. Thereafter Foote signed his name with the title of "Flag-Officer, Commanding Naval Forces Western Waters."

Certainly Foote proved adroit in dealing with his Army counterparts. When Fox wrote him in December, asking about the desirability of transferring the squadron to the Navy Department, Foote responded that while he wished it had been done in the beginning he did not think it wise to do so now. He needed all of his diplomatic skills to deal with Halleck, whom he referred to as a "military imbecile." All this exacted a toll. Foote later confessed to Fox that the experience of preparing the squadron had added ten years to his "age of constitution."

While the more powerful ironclads were being readied, the three wooden gunboats participated in a number of small actions. The *Conestoga*, commanded by Lieutenant Ledyard

Phelps, made regular runs up the Tennessee and Cumberland to monitor Confederate military activity. On October 26, 1861, the *Conestoga* escorted a transport to Eddyville, Kentucky, and early the next morning Federal troops landed, scattering a Rebel force and taking prisoners, mules, and supplies. On December 10 Phelps confirmed that the Confederates were building gunboats on the Cumberland, one at Clarksville and the other at Nashville. He also reported a more powerful vessel, the *Eastport*, under construction up the Tennessee River beyond Fort Henry. Phelps recommended immediate operations on both rivers.

The *Tyler* (Commander Henry Walke) and *Lexington* (Commander Roger N. Stembel), meanwhile, kept guard on the Mississippi below Cairo and reported on the Confederate buildup at Columbus. On September 4 the two steamed downriver to reconnoiter Columbus. Aboard were some of General Grant's staff and a hundred Federal soldiers. Off Columbus, the *Tyler* fired eight to ten 8-inch shells into the Confederate works and then retired. Soon the Union gunboats impressed even Army skeptics.

On November 1, 1861, Frémont ordered Grant to carry out a demonstration against Columbus in order to mask a Federal effort in southeastern Missouri and to prevent Polk from sending reinforcements from Columbus. On November 6 Grant took 3,114 men (five infantry regiments, two guns, and two cavalry companies) down the Mississippi in transports escorted by the *Lexington* and *Tyler*. He had no precise plans when he set out and did not even inform Foote of the operation, but he knew that Columbus was too powerful to assault.

Early on November 7 Grant landed 2,500 men to attack a Confederate force of 2,700 men encamped at Belmont, Missouri, across the Mississippi from the Confederate Gibraltar. The Federal troops went ashore some three miles above Belmont, then moved to attack Confederate positions there, while at Grant's request Commander Walke took his two gunboats to bombard Columbus in a diversionary measure.

As the gunboats circled and exchanged broadsides with the heavy Confederate guns, Grant's men defeated the Confederates ashore. But when they gained the Confederate camp the Federal troops began to loot the area. Polk, meanwhile, sent reinforcements across the river to cut off Grant's men from their transports. But Grant, now outnumbered, succeeded in cutting his way through the Rebels and got most of his men back aboard the transports before the Confederates struck in strength, by which time the Union gunboats had returned. Their grape, canister, and shell, all fired at close range, held off the attackers.

The Battle of Belmont proved costly: 610 Union casualties and 642 Confederate. Both sides claimed victory. General Polk referred to it as a "signal triumph of our arms and the defeat

DON CARLOS BUELL

Born Ohio 1818; raised in Indiana, Buell was graduated from the U.S. Military Academy in 1841, thirty-second in his class of fifty-two; commissioned a 2d lieutenant and posted to infantry, he served against the Seminoles in Florida; promoted to 1st lieutenant during the Mexican War, he also earned two brevets and was seriously wounded at Churubusco; after the war he held a series of staff positions until the outbreak of the Civil War; he was lieutenant colonel and adjutant general of the Department of the Pacific when appointed brigadier general of U.S. Volunteers in May 1861; he commanded a division under General George B. McClellan and helped organize the Army of the Potomac; in November 1861 he assumed command of the Army of the Ohio for a proposed strike into East Tennessee; Buell instead received reluctant authorization to move on the Tennessee capital of Nashville, which his army took with little opposition; promoted to major general

of the machinations of our enemies" and attributed victory to "the favoring providence of Almighty God." Belmont was not an engagement to which Grant could point with particular pride but the North celebrated it as a win, and it delighted Lincoln, who saw in Grant a general willing to fight. Hardly the beginning of a great thrust down the Mississippi as depicted in the Northern press, Belmont did help bring about Federal control of Missouri and provided valuable combat experience for Grant's troops. The Navy certainly had reason to be pleased; it had demonstrated that it could speed the movement of men and supplies, operate with surprise and flexibility, and provide effective artillery support for troops ashore.

Early in January 1862 General McClellan ordered Grant, through Halleck, to stage a "demonstration" in the direction of Nashville. McClellan assumed that Buell was about to begin

U.S.V. in March 1862; moving to join General U.S. Grant's army at Pittsburg Landing, Buell's force arrived late on the first day of the Battle of Shiloh; on the second day the combined armies of Buell and Grant drove the Confederates from the field; during the campaign against Corinth, Buell led the Army of the Ohio under the overall command of General Henry Halleck; ordered in June 1862 to advance on Chattanooga, Buell was stymied by Confederate resistance; promoted to colonel in the regular establishment in July 1862; forced to withdraw into Kentucky to oppose the Confederate invasion of that state, he turned back General Braxton Bragg's army at Perryville in October, but failed to pursue aggressively the retreating Confederates; for this failure he was relieved of his command; while a military commission reviewed his performance he remained without orders for more than a year; although the commission brought no charges, Buell was mustered out of the Volunteers in May 1864; a month later he resigned his regular commission; he settled in Kentucky, where he operated an ironworks and coal mine; he died at his Kentucky home in 1898. General Buell possessed undeniable administrative talents and was capable of solid battlefield leadership; his ouster perhaps owed more to his close friendship with McClellan and the rise of Grant than to his performance.

his long-delayed offensive on Nashville and hoped that such a "demonstration," accompanied by appropriate publicity, would keep the Confederates at Columbus and those at Forts Henry and Donelson from reinforcing Brigadier General Simon Bolivar Buckner's command at Bowling Green.

Grant ordered C. F. Smith at Paducah to send troops up the western bank of the Tennessee River to threaten Fort Henry. At the same time he accompanied 6,000 men of Brigadier General John A. McClernand's Division from Cairo and Bird's Point into western Kentucky to threaten Columbus.

The weather was cold with rain and snow; the roads, never very good in the best of times, were horrible. Despite the elements, Grant's mission of more than a week was a success, providing further training for his men and preventing Confederate troop movements.

The gunboats also were busy. The *Conestoga* and *Lexington* supported Smith from the Tennessee, while the *Essex* and *St. Louis* did the same for McClernand on the Mississippi. On January 11 the latter two fought an hour-long battle with three Confederate gunboats that came up from Columbus in which the Federal gunboats prevailed.

Buell and Halleck were still at loggerheads over strategy. Buell opposed any large-scale attack by Halleck against Fort Henry. He informed both Halleck and McClellan that he could support Grant only by marching his entire army against Bowling Green, something he was not prepared to do. Anything less, he said, would be unsuccessful and taken by the Confederates as a mere demonstration.

Under pressure from both McClellan and Lincoln for an assault into eastern Tennessee, Buell did finally send Brigadier General George H. Thomas with 4,000 men on the upper Cumberland River in a thrust toward Knoxville. Confederate Major General George B. Crittenden and Brigadier General Felix Zollicoffer with some 4,000 troops dangerously positioned at Beech Grove on the north bank of the Cumberland

River, seventy miles northwest of Cumberland Gap, soon learned of Thomas' activity. Crittenden, who did not want to risk a retreat across the flooded Cumberland under attack, chose instead to confront Thomas. This led to the January 19 Battle of Logan's Cross Roads (or Mill Springs), in which Thomas displayed superior generalship driving the Confederates back to Beech Grove, where they crossed the river during the night and fell back on Cumberland Gap. The victory, in which Zollicoffer lost his life, shattered Johnston's right flank, and changed Union strategy in the West.

With Eastern Kentucky now under Federal control, Buell, citing poor roads and supply difficulties, did not follow up the victory by advancing into eastern Tennessee. Thomas moved his division to Burkesville, Kentucky, about seventy-five miles northeast of Nashville on the Cumberland. Both he and Buell wanted Foote's gunboats to push up the Cumberland past Fort Donelson, destroy the railroad bridge at Clarksville, then rendezvous with Thomas' troops at Burkesville for an attack on Nashville. The generals believed this was preferable to an operation under Halleck against Fort Henry.

After McClellan rejected Buell's proposal, Buell suggested a full-scale attack against Bowling Green in conjunction with Halleck's descent on Fort Henry. But Buell's troops did not move from Burkesville until February 6, far too late to effect the strategic concentration that Halleck sought.

Halleck, who opposed multiple lines of operation, favored concentrating in middle Tennessee, with Buell within supporting distance. He wanted to attack Fort Henry at the same time that Buell moved against Fort Donelson. Concentrating Union strength in the vicinity of the two forts would also mean that Halleck could turn Columbus without having to attack that stronghold. McClellan agreed that securing control of Confederate rail lines emanating from Nashville was much more important than taking Columbus or Memphis.

While the two department commanders were conferring

with McClellan rather than each other, General Smith's column, accompanied up the Tennessee by the *Conestoga*, *Lexington*, and *Tyler*, got to within 2.5 miles of Forts Heiman and Henry. This convinced Smith that the Confederate forts were vulnerable to capture by a combined land and river operation. Uncompleted Fort Heiman occupied the high ground commanding Fort Henry from the other side of the Tennessee River. As Grant noted later,

> Its possession by us, with the aid of our gunboats, would insure the capture of Fort Henry. This report of Smith confirmed views I had previously held, that the true line of operations for us was up the Tennessee and Cumberland rivers. With us there, the enemy would be compelled to fall back on the east and west entirely out of the State of Kentucky.

Grant was eager to get on with a major campaign. He wrote his sister that he now commanded more men than Winfield Scott had in Mexico and that he hoped to "retain so important a command for at least one battle." On January 6 he secured grudging permission from Halleck to visit him in St. Louis in order to discuss important military matters, actually to persuade him to launch an immediate offensive in which troops would be moved by river against Fort Henry and then invade the Tennessee River Valley. As Grant recalled, Halleck received him with "so little cordiality that I perhaps stated the object of my visit with less clearness than I might have done, and I had not uttered many sentences before I was cut short as if my plan was preposterous. I returned to Cairo very much crestfallen."

Grant may have failed to win Halleck's approval, but the idea did not die. A number of people later claimed credit for conceiving the river campaign against Forts Henry and Donelson. Navy Commander William D. Porter had reported the vulnerability of Fort Henry to naval attack and Lieutenant

Phelps had urged an assault on both the Cumberland and
Tennessee Rivers. Buell had also advocated it and Smith had
pointed out the vulnerability of Fort Henry. But the most per-
sistent advocates of such a campaign were Grant and Foote.
The two men consulted often and as Grant put it, "he agreed
with me perfectly as to the feasibility of the campaign up the
Tennessee." Foote remembered it a bit differently: "I proposed
to General Grant . . . that with four of the boats and 6,000
troops we should ascend the Tennessee and attack Fort Henry.
The General preferred the Cumberland and Fort Donelson, as
the more appropriate points of attack, but yielded to my views
if General Halleck's assent could be obtained." Certainly Foote
chafed under Halleck's inaction. He wrote Welles that "little
progress could be made towards taking Vicksburg, opening the
Mississippi and subduing the insurrection" with Halleck in
active command.

Foote and Grant could hardly have been more different. The
one was God-fearing, an anti-slavery advocate, and tetotaling;
the other may have feared God, but he was certainly indiffer-
ent toward slavery and hardly abstemious. Still, the two men
worked together splendidly. The subsequent success of the
river campaign in Tennessee owed much to this positive rela-
tionship and to the two leaders' initiative and leadership.

On January 22, 1862, Grant received Smith's formal report
on the vulnerability of Forts Heiman and Henry. Convinced of
the report's accuracy, Grant on January 28 renewed his call
for an offensive, telegraphing Halleck: "With permission, I will
take Fort Henry, on the Tennessee and establish and hold a
large camp there." Foote concurred in another telegram:
"General Grant and myself are of the opinion that Fort Henry,
on the Tennessee River, can be carried with four ironclad gunboats and troops, and be permanently occupied. Have we your
authority to move for that purpose when ready?" The next day
Grant sent a detailed proposal by letter.

Whether or not Foote's support was decisive, Halleck probably saw the need to counter Buell's success in Kentucky. Also, on January 27 Lincoln, using his authority as commander-in-chief of the nation's armed forces, had issued General War Order Number 1, in which he decreed that all Union armies begin an advance on February 22 (George Washington's birthday and Jefferson Davis' inauguration day). Perhaps the final straw in prompting Halleck was a report that Richmond had sent Confederate reinforcements west. As Halleck relayed it to Grant, "A telegram from Washington says that Beauregard left Manassas four days ago with fifteen regiments for the line of Columbus and Bowling Green. It is therefore of the greatest importance that we cut that line before he arrives. You will move with the least delay possible." Unfortunately for General Johnston and the Confederacy the report was true only to the extent that Beauregard indeed was on the way; the reinforcement was limited to a handful of staff officers.

For all these reasons on January 30 Halleck wired Grant, "Make your preparations to take and hold Fort Henry. I will send you written instructions by mail." The expedition started on February 2. Johnston's bluff was about to be called.

3

THE CAPTURE OF FORT HENRY

After Tennessee's secession from the Union, Governor Isham G. Harris sent former West Pointer Brigadier General Daniel S. Donelson as part of a commission to select sites along the Tennessee and Cumberland Rivers for fortifications. Although Donelson reported no good locations, he did choose two. One on the Tennessee River was named Fort Henry for Gustavus A. Henry, the state's senior Confederate senator. The other, on the Cumberland, was named for the general himself.

In the summer of 1861 Colonel Adolphus Heiman and the 720 men of his 10th Tennessee Infantry Regiment began work on the Tennessee River site. Fort Henry covered some three acres of ground in a solidly built five-sided earthwork parapet about eight feet high. Rifle pits extended to the river and along the water and from outside of Fort Henry's perimeter some two miles to the east toward Dover and Fort Donelson.

In December 1861 Brigadier General Lloyd Tilghman

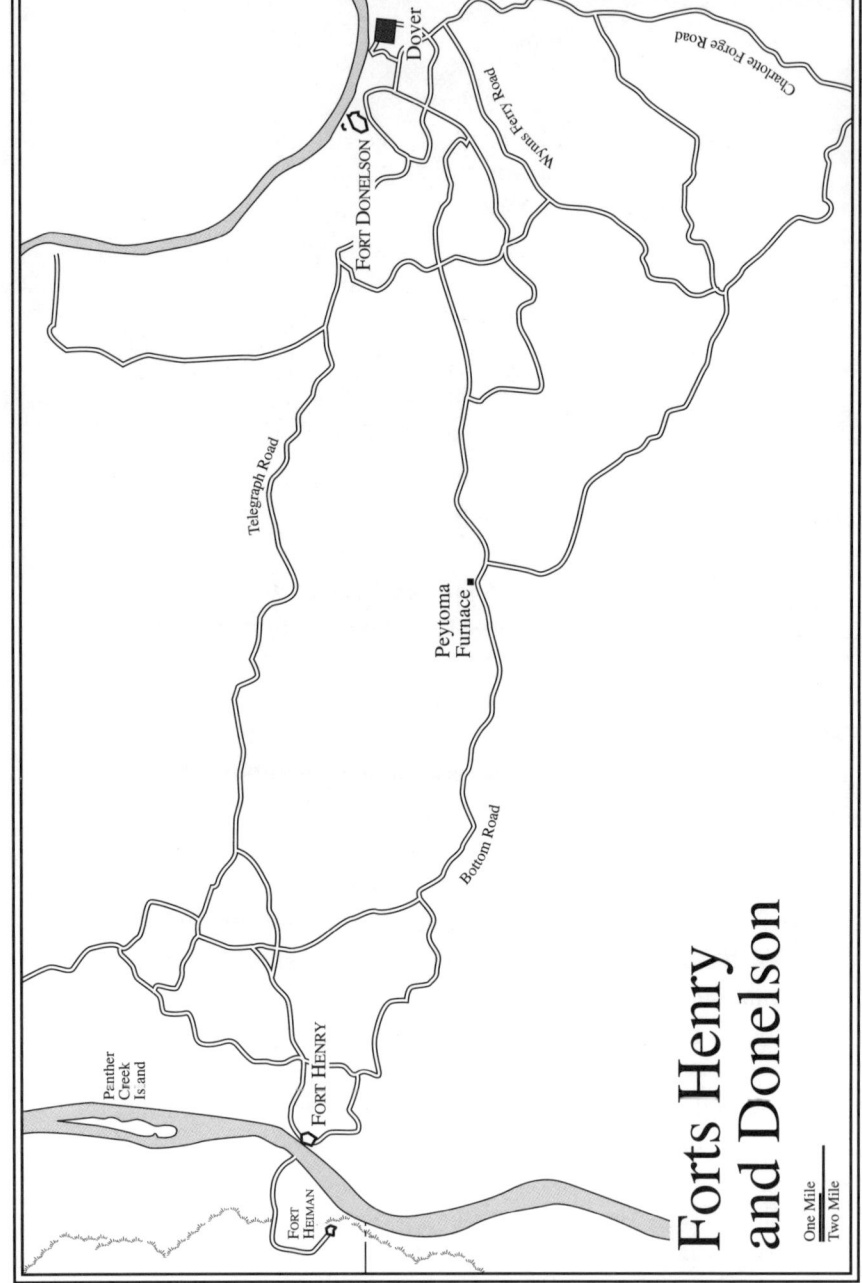

Forts Henry
and Donelson

assumed command of Forts Henry and Donelson. An 1836 West Point graduate, Tilghman's only active military duty had been during the Mexican War. He and others who served at Fort Henry were as one in criticizing its location.

Although it lay in a bend of the Tennessee River and commanded a straight stretch of water some three miles long, Henry was on low ground washed by the river. Artillery Captain Jesse Taylor wrote: "we had a more dangerous force to contend with than the Federals,—namely the river itself." The fort also was commanded by higher terrain on both sides. When Johnston's military engineers finally examined Fort Henry they found it to be badly located and confirmed that it could be dominated by high ground across the river. Johnston then ordered that high ground be fortified and held. Tilghman later called Henry "a wretched military position," adding:

> I should explain fully the unfortunate location of Fort Henry in reference to resistance by a small force against an attack by land co-operating with the gunboats, as well as its disadvantages in even an engagement with boats alone. The entire fort . . . is enfiladed from three or four points on the opposite shore, while three points on the eastern bank completely command them both, all at easy cannon range. . . . The history of military engineering records no parallel to this case. Points within a few miles of it, possessing great advantages and few disadvantages, were totally neglected, and a location fixed upon without one redeeming feature or filling one of the many requirements of a site for a work such as Fort Henry. . . . An enemy had but to use their most common sense in obtaining the advantage of high water, as was the case, to have complete and entire control of the position.

Tilghman, apparently, was dilatory in efforts to rectify the situation. By January he had barely started construction on the heights above the west bank of what was known as Fort Heiman after Fort Henry's second in command. Having ordered the work done months before, Johnston was furious. Although he telegraphed Tilghman to intensify efforts to entrench

LLOYD TILGHMAN

Born Maryland 1816; Tilghman was graduated from the U.S. Military Academy in 1836, forty-sixth in his class of forty-nine; posted to the 1st Dragoons, the resigned his 2d lieutenant's commission only weeks later to become a railroad engineer; during the War with Mexico, he served on the staff of General David Twiggs and as a captain in the Maryland and District of Columbia Battalion; following the war he returned to railroad engineering, mostly in Panama; in 1852 he settled in Kentucky, where he was active in the state's military organization; following the outbreak of the Civil War, Tilghman offered his services to the Confederacy and was appointed brigadier general in October 1861; assigned to Kentucky, he grew concerned over the tenuous nature of Confederate defenses on the Tennessee and Cumberland Rivers; charged with improving the works at Forts Henry and Donelson, he found his authority encumbered and the process frustrating; when Union Flag Officer Andrew Foote's gunboats approached Fort Henry in February 1862, Tilghman sent most of the garrison to Fort Donelson, and with some 100 men put up a spirited defense, often serving the guns himself, before surrendering; not exchanged until August 1862, he commanded rendezvous and instruction camps before heading a brigade at Corinth and in the retreat from Holly Springs; during the Vicksburg Campaign, he commanded a brigade in General W.W. Loring's Division; in the fighting at Champion Hill, again personally working a cannon, Tilghman was killed when a Federal shell fragment tore through his body; a magnificent equestrian statue on the grounds of Vicksburg National Military Park commemorates the general's last stand.

Heiman, work there was unfinished when the Federals arrived.

By February 1862 Fort Henry mounted seventeen heavy guns: twelve facing the river and five guarding the land approaches. The fort had eight 32-pounders, two 42-pounders, one 128-pounder Columbiad rifled gun, five long 18-pounder siege guns, and a 6-inch rifled gun (also described as a 24-pounder caliber throwing a 68-pound shot). There were also six old 12-pounders. Suspicious of the latter, the defenders tested two of them, which blew up. They promptly discarded the others.

Compounding problems for the Confederates, in early February 1862 both the Tennessee and Cumberland rivers were in flood. At Fort Henry the high water came near to flooding magazines and to within a few feet of the guns themselves; some of the land within the fort's perimeter was two feet under water. Also the Confederates lacked ammunition for their 42-pounders, leaving only nine guns able to counter a water approach. And Tilghman had only 2,610 men in two brigades under Colonels Heiman and Joseph Drake. Many of the defenders were raw recruits armed only with shotguns and hunting rifles. Men of the 10th Tennessee carried old flintlocks that dated from the War of 1812.

Area roads were very poor, so Grant moved his entire force to Fort Henry by water. While he could use numerous steamers laid up at Cairo because the Mississippi was closed to navigation beyond that point, there were still not enough of them or men to operate them to move at once all of the 17,000 men Grant planned to take with him. Two troop lifts would be required.

On February 2 the first lift of men moved up the Tennessee. Although in January the ironclads had been sent to Cairo and great effort had been made to ready them for service, only four were ready when the expedition set out: the *Cincinnati* (flagship, Commander Stembel), *Carondelet* (Commander Walke), *Essex* (Commander Porter), and *St. Louis* (Lieutenant Leonard Paulding). Eads had been prompt in building them, but

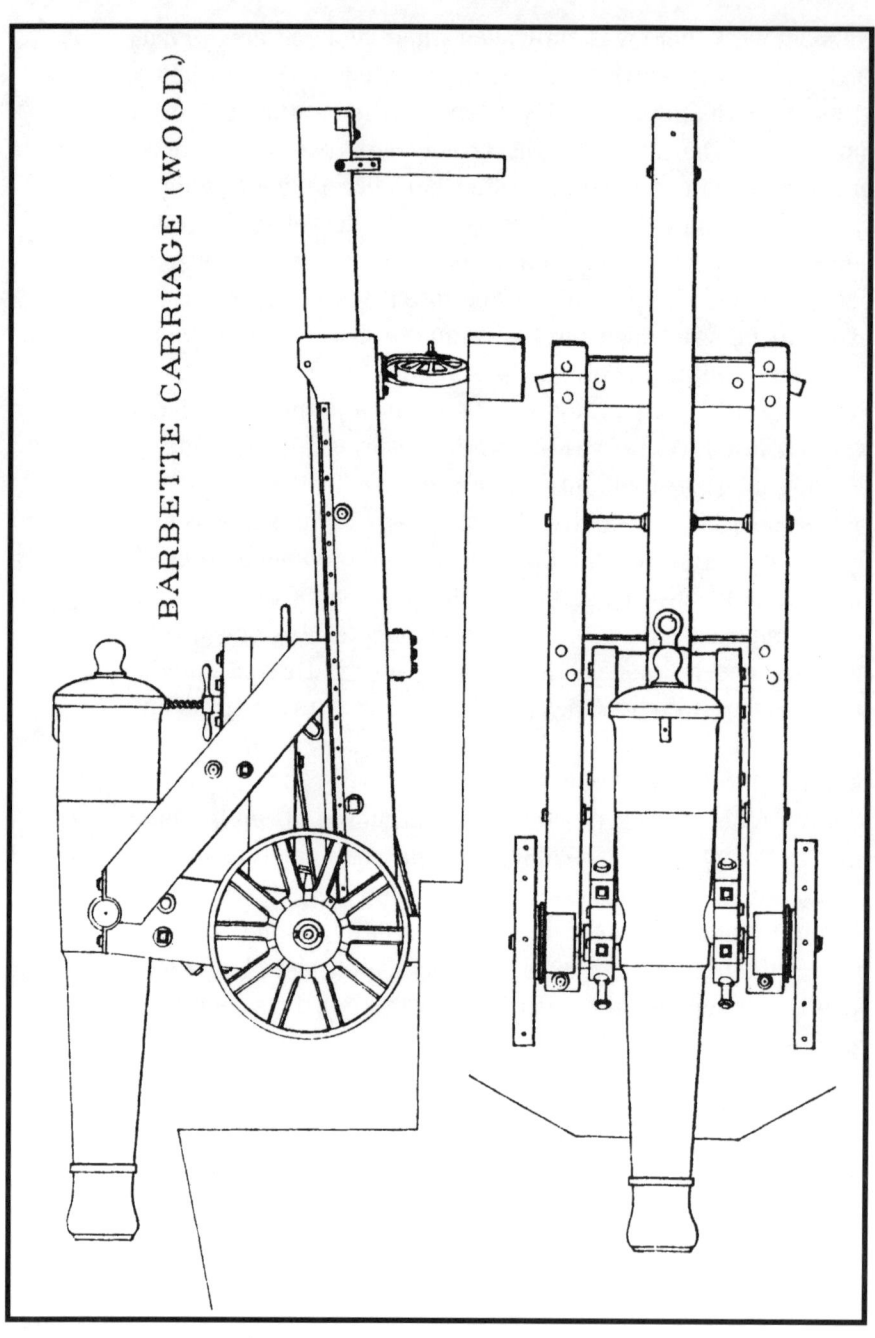

BARBETTE CARRIAGE (WOOD.)

Washington had not been as prompt in paying for them. When the gunboats set out for Henry, therefore, Eads had not been reimbursed, so technically they were still his property.

The ironclads led the advance up the Tennessee while the more vulnerable timberclads, the *Conestoga* (Lieutenant S. Ledyard Phelps), *Tyler* (Lieutenant William Gwin), and *Lexington* (Lieutenant James W. Shirk) kept to the rear. Although the strong river current made for slow and dangerous progress, it did sweep away a number of Confederate torpedoes(the contemporary term for mine). Foote had serious doubts about the mortar boats, including their construction and stability and the difficulty of towing them against a strong current, but all for naught, because the mortars did not arrive in time and the boats were left behind.

Grant had given command of the expedition to General McClernand and followed in one of the later boats. On February 4 McClernand halted some six miles below (north of) Fort Henry.

The Confederates soon spread the alarm. At 4:00 PM on the 4th a courier rode into Fort Donelson with word from Colonel Heiman at Fort Henry that at 4:30 AM signal rockets from a picket at Bailey's Landing on the Tennessee had announced the approach of gunboats. Tilghman, who had been working to improve the defenses at Donelson, immediately left to take direction of Fort Henry's defense. Lieutenant Colonel Jeremy F. Gilmer, chief engineer of the Western Department sent by Johnston to try to remedy deficiencies in the defenses of Henry and Donelson, went with Tilghman, as did some cavalry. Captain Taylor, commanding Fort Henry's artillery, recalled, "Far as eye could see, the course of the river could be traced by the dense volumes of smoke issuing from the flotilla—indicating that the long-threatened attempt to break our lines was to be made in earnest."

Upon his arrival at the Federal anchorage Grant wanted to know how close he could land his men to Fort Henry without putting them under fire. He boarded the *Essex* and proceeded upriver past the mouth of Panther Creek, which flowed westward into the Tennessee. Because of heavy rains the river was out of its banks. The creek was a torrent and Grant hoped he could land south of it. The *Essex* soon came under fire but the shots fell short. Grant had decided he could land safely south of Panther Creek when the Confederates opened up with a rifled gun that outranged those aboard the ironclad. James Laning, second mate aboard the ironclad, described what happened:

> When about two, or two and a half miles distant, the fort fired a rifle shot, which passed over our boat to the right and cut down a number of saplings on shore. In a few moments, another shot, fired with more precision, passed over the spar-deck among the officers; through the officers' quarters, visiting in its flight the steerage, commander's pantry and cabin, passing through the stern; doing, however, no damage except breaking some of the captain's dishes, and cutting the feet from a pair of his socks, which happened to be hanging over the back of a chair in his cabin. These shots reaching us at so great a distance, rather astonished us, as the enemy intended they should.

This shot barely missed both Grant and Porter and caused Porter to turn back immediately. Grant then ordered the troops debarked north of Panther Creek at Bailey's Ferry, three miles from the fort and just beyond the range of its guns.

On February 4, as Federal troops went ashore to work their way through the swamps and encircle the fort, Foote put the crews of the *Tyler* and *Conestoga* to work searching for torpedoes; they soon removed six from the river. Grant, meanwhile, left for Paducah with the empty transports to hurry along Smith's Division. He returned the next day with Smith's advance elements.

Late on the 5th, three of the gunboats steamed into view of Fort Henry and opened a "vigorous and well-directed fire," which killed one defender and wounded three others. It also prompted the Confederates to fire six shots in return, at which point the gunboats withdrew.

The entire Federal command was not ashore until the night of the 5th, when it rained heavily. Although he did not yet have all his men in place, Grant believed the Confederates quickly would move to reinforce Fort Henry. As he recalled, "prompt action on our part was imperative." That evening, hopeful that all his men would have arrived in time, Grant ordered the advance to begin at 11:00 AM the next day.

Foote, meanwhile, inspected his ships and admonished the men. James Laning aboard the *Essex* remembered that the flag officer told the crew "to be brave and courageous, and above all to place their faith in Divine Providence." He instructed Laning, who had charge of the gunboat's battery, to make every shot count:

> [his] greatest efforts should be to disable the enemy's guns, and to be sure you do not throw any ammunition away. Every charge you fire from one of those guns cost the government about eight dollars. If your shots fall short you encourage the enemy. If they reach home you demoralize him, and get the worth of your money.

Grant planned a simultaneous land and water attack. During the night of the 5th he sent General Smith with two of his brigades along the west bank of the river to prevent reinforcement from that direction, to cut off any Confederate escape, and to seize the high ground at Fort Heiman for possible artillery emplacement. Smith's men discovered the Confederates had already evacuated Heiman.

The main Union land effort was on the east bank of the river by McClernand's Division with a brigade from Smith's.

But the area's wretched roads, dense woods, and swampy conditions prolonged the advance on Fort Henry.

Grant need not have worried because the Confederates were not reinforcing Fort Henry. On the 4th Tilghman had telegraphed General Polk for reinforcements and on the next day he optimistically stated "there was a glorious chance to overwhelm the enemy." But no reinforcements arrived.

On the night of the 5th, realizing the strength of the Federal forces and well aware of the long odds he faced, Tilghman called together his principal officers. They were pessimistic, believing that they could not withstand attack by an enemy force estimated to number at least 25,000 men. Tilghman then asked Captain Taylor if his guns could "hold out for one hour against a determined attack." When Taylor replied in the affirmative, Tilghman ordered his commanders to have their men ready to move at a "moment's notice."

At 10:00 on the morning of the 6th, before the Federal attack began, Tilghman ordered his troops, except the artillerymen who manned the fort's batteries, to move to Fort Donelson. This left at Henry, including those too sick to move, only about a hundred soldiers. Tilghman saw the men on their way to safety and then returned to the fort to share its fate. He hoped to delay the attackers long enough for most of his command to escape.

By the time Tilghman returned to Henry the naval attack was already underway. At 10:20 AM Foote signaled his squadron to prepare for battle, and at 10:50 he ordered the ships to proceed. At 11:35 the four ironclads formed in line abreast. The *Essex* was on the right, then the *Cincinnati*, *Carondelet*, and *St. Louis*. Because of the narrowness of the river the last two gunboats were lashed together and remained so during the battle. A half-mile behind them came the division of timberclads—the *Conestoga*, *Lexington*, and *Tyler*—under Lieutenant Phelps. As the squadron neared Fort Henry there was no sound from ashore and no sign of Union troops. Foote

then decided to begin the battle alone. The fort with its
Confederate flag, huts, and earthworks soon came into view.

At 11:45, from a range of about 1,700 yards, the *Cincinnati*
fired a shot that signaled the other gunboats to commence. At
about a mile's range Taylor ordered the water battery to
respond; the firing then became general. The gunboats used
only their bow guns, initially elevated at seven degrees with
shell fuses set to explode at fifteen seconds. The gunboats
continued to fire as they closed to within 600 yards of the fort,
when their guns were depressed to only three degrees and
shells set at a five-second delay. Phelps' division remained at

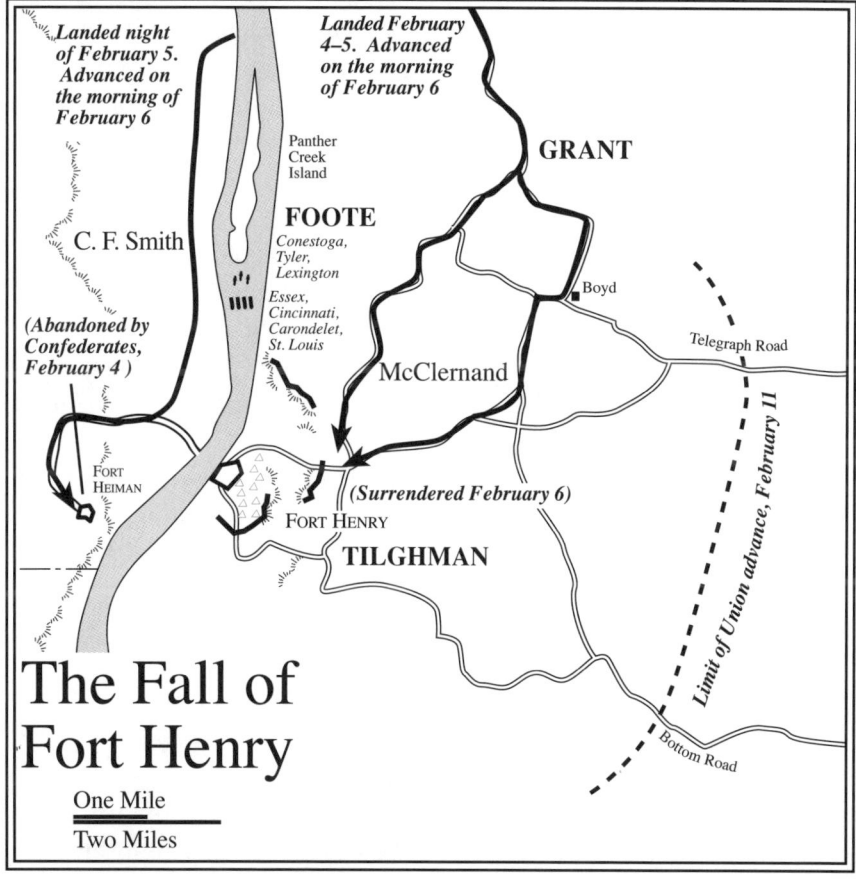

Landed night
of February 5.
Advanced on
the morning of
February 6

Landed February
4–5. Advanced
on the morning
of February 6

Panther
Creek
Island

GRANT

C. F. Smith

FOOTE
Conestoga,
Tyler,
Lexington
Essex,
Cincinnati,
Carondelet,
St. Louis

Boyd

(Abandoned by
Confederates,
February 4)

Telegraph Road

McClernand

FORT
HEIMAN

(Surrendered February 6)

FORT HENRY

TILGHMAN

Limit of Union advance, February 11

The Fall of
Fort Henry

One Mile

Two Miles

Bottom Road

long range lobbing shells into the fort.

Captain Taylor ordered each Confederate gun crew to concentrate on a particular vessel. The Confederates had an advantage in knowing precise ranges to their targets and their fire was both lively and accurate. Although Fort Henry had only nine guns that could respond, the Rebel gunners succeeded in hitting all of the gunboats many times (fifty-nine hits in all) but most of the damage was slight, except on the *Essex*.

About two thirds of the way through the battle and after the *Essex* had fired seventy-two shots from its two 9-inch Dahlgren shell guns, a Confederate shell tore into the middle boiler of the ironclad. The blast and resulting steam killed or wounded thirty-two officers and men, including Commander Porter who was badly scalded. Out of control, the gunboat drifted downriver. Another seamen was killed and nine more wounded on board the *Cincinnati*, and one man aboard the *Essex* was killed by a musket ball.

There was more damage ashore. From the beginning, Union fire was very accurate, and the crews could see shell explosions throw up earth around the Rebel guns. At 12:35 the 6-inch rifled gun blew up, killing or wounding all its crew, and a priming wire stuck in the vent of the 10-inch Columbiad, effectively spiking it. Two 32-pounders were then struck at almost the same time and, as Taylor described it, "the flying fragments of the shattered guns and bursted shells disabled every man at the two guns." Confederate gunners grew dispirited and even the example of Tilghmam working one of the guns himself failed to elicit much enthusiasm.

Lieutenant Colonel Gilmer and some others now escaped for Donelson. With only four guns able to return fire, at 1:50 PM Tilghman mounted the parapet and waved a flag of truce. Heavy smoke prevented Federal gunners from seeing this but five minutes later Captain Taylor and a sergeant succeeded in freeing the halyards on the flagpole and lowered the Confederate flag. Taylor reported that the gunboats were only two hundred yards from the fort and sweeping it with their fire.

Tilghman sent his adjutant out in a small boat to the *Cincinnati*, and Foote then sent ashore Lieutenants Stembel and Phelps to raise the U.S. colors. Phelps took the surrender ashore from Captain Taylor, who represented Tilghman. Later, at Foote's request, Tilghman went aboard the flagship.

The Confederate gunners had done their jobs and gained two hours for their compatriots to escape. Only ninety-four men, including Tilghman and sixteen men aboard a hospital boat *Patton*, surrendered at Henry. Confederate personnel losses from Federal fire were remarkably light: five killed, eleven wounded, and five missing. The victors captured the fort's heavy guns, plus supplies and equipment abandoned by the departed garrison, which had retreated to Donelson in haste and on foot without wagons.

By the time Grant's troops arrived the battle was over. McClernand had moved out with his division on schedule at 11:00 AM, followed by Smith's third brigade. Grant had ordered him to get astride the road to Fort Donelson and Dover in order to prevent Confederate troops from reinforcing Fort Henry or evacuating it. He was then to await Grant's orders and be ready to storm Henry if need be. Poor road conditions—the track was mired in mud—delayed the troops' arrival, but they cheered the sound of the naval bombardment. At 3:00 PM McClernand learned that the Confederates might be evacuating the fort and sent cavalry ahead to verify this. The Federal troopers pursued the retreating Confederates, slowed by muddy roads, for some three miles and managed to capture six guns and thirty-eight stragglers before giving up the chase. About an hour after the fort's surrender the first Union troops arrived. Lieutenant Walke, whom Foote had placed in charge, then turned Fort Henry over to Grant.

Back East, McClellan was delighted with the news. He wired Halleck, "Please thank Grant and Foote and their commands for me." His request was carried out only with respect to Foote.

After the fall of Fort Henry, Grant called together his officers to discuss the possibility of taking Donelson. "The question for consideration, gentlemen, is," Grant informed them, "whether we shall march against Fort Donelson or wait for reinforcements. I should like to have your views." All favored a move against Donelson as soon as possible.

4
FORT DONELSON

Fort Donelson was located on the west bank of the
Cumberland River two miles north of the little county seat of
Dover, which Federal General Lew Wallace later referred to as
"a village unknown to fame, meager in population, architec-
turally poor." But the fort was both larger and better placed
than Henry.

Fort Donelson occupied a steep bluff as much as a hundred
feet above the Cumberland and commanded a straight stretch
of river for several miles. The fort was bounded by two
streams north and south: Hickman Creek on the north and
what would normally constitute a ravine, known as Indian
Creek, to the south. Both emptied into the Cumberland. Small
branches feeding into these creeks had carved out a series of
ridgelines fifty to eighty feet high paralleling the river up
which an attacker from the land side would have to charge.

Because the Cumberland was then in flood, the creeks

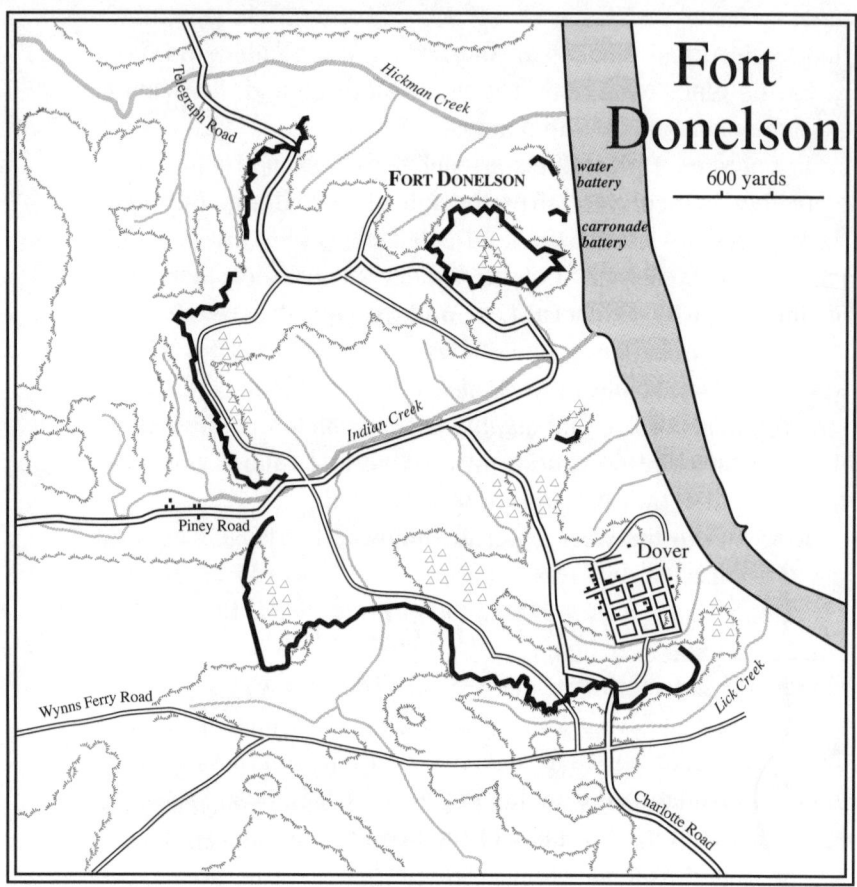

opening onto it were filled with deep water and were much wider than normal. This aided the defenders by providing a natural barrier but also worked to the advantage of attackers in that they would not have to extend their longer, exterior, line to cover these points of the line. Also, the backwater up Indian Creek within the wider Confederate defensive lines bisected their position and made communication with Dover difficult.

The fort itself was only about fifteen acres in size. Constructed by troops and slaves over a period of some seven months, it had earthen works at least six feet high. Over time the garrison had built some four hundred log cabins as barracks. Its outer works covered much more ground, by Grant's estimate about one hundred acres.

In February 1862 Donelson's defenses were not quite complete, but immediately after the fall of Fort Henry the men there pushed to extend the land defenses. On his arrival from Fort Henry, Lieutenant-Colonel Gilmer supervised placement of rifle pits, which General Lew Wallace later described as "a continuous but irregular line of logs, covered with yellow clay." New arrivals were set to work clearing timber to secure unobstructed fields of fire and digging entrenchments. Additionally, the men took the precaution of cooking three days' worth of rations in case they had to retreat to Nashville.

Rifle pits to the west generally followed the ridgelines and reached out some two miles beyond Dover toward Fort Henry. The ground itself was hilly and generally wooded. Beyond the entrenched line over about half of its length was a ravine running north and south that opened onto Hickman Creek. On the fort side of this ravine the defenders cut trees down to about chest high, leaving them attached to their stumps with the tops pointed outward from the entrenchments. These formed a crude abatis in front of most of the Confederate line and made access from the land side quite difficult.

Donelson's guns were well sited. Its two river batteries were cut into the slope of the ridge facing northward downriver. The most important of these was the lower site, the one farthest to the north. Thanks to a slight bend in the river, it commanded a view of the Cumberland beyond the extreme range of its guns. It consisted of a trench some twenty feet wide dug in the hillside, some thirty feet above river level at the time of the battle. Excavated dirt was mounded up on the lower side of the slope to make a rampart some twelve feet high. Carefully positioned sandbags added to its height and were placed so as to leave narrow embrasures for the guns

Upper Water Battery, Fort Donelson

These could be slight because the river targets against which the guns would fire would be on a narrow front. The trench was also arranged so that each gun was protected from the one next to it. These traverses insured that an explosion at one gun would not affect others. This battery contained the defenders' largest gun, a 10-inch Columbiad on a barbette mount, and nine 32-pounders.

The upper battery, to the south of the first and directly east of the fort, also could fire upriver. It contained three guns: a 10-inch Columbiad in exterior appearance but bored and rifled as a 32-pounder and firing a conical 128-pound round, and two 32-pounder carronades, short guns designed for close-range fire. The fort itself had eight additional guns. Admiral David D. Porter later described Donelson as "the strongest military work in the entire theater of war."

The day after the fall of Fort Henry Brigadier General Bushrod R. Johnson assumed command at Donelson. Its garrison then numbered only about 6,000 men, including the two brigades of infantry that had fled Fort Henry under Colonel Heiman and had arrived the night of the 6th.

In reporting the loss of Fort Henry to Richmond, Johnston assumed Grant would move next on Donelson and that it would probably fall to the gunboats alone:

> The slight resistance at Fort Henry indicates that the best open earthworks are not reliable to meet success-fully a vigorous attack of iron-clad gunboats, and, although now supported by a considerable force, I think the gunboats of the enemy will probably take Fort Donelson without the necessity of employing their land force in co-operation, as seems to have been done at Fort Henry."

When Johnston, Beauregard, and Major General William J. Hardee met at Bowling Green to consider their options after the fall of Fort Henry all agreed that Donelson could not be held. Johnston saw the need to extract his forward defenders so the army could fight under more favorable circumstances. Kentucky would be given up for the time being and Confederate forces at Bowling Green, now the eastern anchor of the Confederate defensive line, would retreat on Nashville for a defense behind the Cumberland. Except for a small force, Columbus would also be evacuated and its troops withdrawn to Humboldt, Tennessee. Efforts would also be made to hold Island No. 10 and Fort Pillow, both on the Mississippi upriver from Memphis. In a message to Richmond, Johnston reported that all three generals agreed on these moves.

Beauregard later claimed that he had urged Johnston to concentrate Confederate resources at Donelson. Although this claim went unsubstantiated, on February 14 Beauregard did write prophetically, "We must give up some minor points, and concentrate our forces to save the most important ones, or we will lose all of them in succession."

BUSHROD R. JOHNSON

Born Ohio 1817; graduated from the U.S. Military Academy in 1840, twenty-third in his class of forty-two that included W.T. Sherman, G.H. Thomas, and R.S. Ewell; commissioned 2d lieutenant and posted to the 3d Infantry, he served on the frontier, in the Seminole War, and in Mexico; promoted to 1st lieutenant in February 1844; he resigned his commission in 1847 to become an educator; an instructor and administrator at the Western Military Institute in Kentucky and the Military College of the University of Nashville, Johnson was also active in both the Kentucky and Tennessee militias; he entered Confederate service as a colonel of engineers in June 1861 and was appointed brigadier general the following January; forced to surrender with the garrison at Fort Donelson in February 1862, he managed to escape through Union lines; wounded while leading a brigade at Shiloh, he recovered to lead his brigade in General Braxton Bragg's invasion of Kentucky and at Murfreesboro; commanded a provisional division at Chickamauga and directed General Simon B. Buckner's Division at Knoxville; transferred to the Eastern Theater, he led a brigade in the early defense of Petersburg; promoted to major general, he commanded a division in the Petersburg trenches and took part in restoring the Confederate line during the Battle of the Crater in July 1864; relieved of duty after his division was destroyed at Sayler's Creek in April 1865, he was without a command when he surrendered at Appomattox; after the war he became chancellor of the University of Nashville. General Johnson died at his farm near Brighton, Illinois, in 1880.

Johnston did not go to Donelson; he was determined to lead the troops at Bowling Green to safety. But if Johnston believed Donelson was untenable, why did he send 12,000 reinforcements to the fort? This force was not big enough to defeat Grant and would merely up the number of Confederate captives once the fort fell to the Federals.

Johnston thought that reinforcing Donelson would keep Grant at bay until he could withdraw the rest of his eastern forces to Nashville; in fact, he informed Jefferson Davis of his intention to fight for Nashville at Donelson. As Union General Lew Wallace noted, despite knowledge of vast Union forces opposing him, Johnston, "persisted in fighting for Nashville, and for that purpose he divided his thirty thousand men. Fourteen thousand he kept in observation of Buell at Louisville. Sixteen thousand he gave to defend Fort Donelson. The latter detachment he himself called, "'the best part of his army.'" It is difficult to think of a great master of strategy making an error so perilous."

If indeed he was determined to make a stand at Donelson, Johnston might have concentrated all his available forces there, instead, of dividing his effort and sending half of the available men to Donelson and the other half to Nashville. Grant certainly believed Johnston made a major blunder. He had considered Johnston a formidable opponent but, he later admitted, "after studying the orders and dispatches of Johnston, I am compelled to materially modify my views of that officer's qualifications as a soldier. My judgment now is that he was vacillating and undecided in his actions." Such behavior could be fatal against an aggressive commander such as Grant.

Had Johnston concentrated all his resources in the north at Donelson he could have confronted Grant's 15,000 invaders with 30,000 men before Buell arrived with reinforcements. With Grant defeated, Buell would have had to retreat back to the Ohio. But the Confederate high command failed to think of their separate detachments as part of a whole. The Confederates were also handicapped by the fact that their forces west of the Mississippi, lacking rail connections with the remainder of the department, fought their own separate war. Johnston could also have left Hardee to supervise the retreat from Bowling Green and gone to Donelson himself or sent Beauregard. Instead he took charge of the retreat from Bowling Green and sent Beauregard to supervise the Confederate withdrawal from Columbus.

Importantly, Johnston was able to shift so many men to Donelson because Buell was slow to move and too far north to pose an immediate threat. Johnston hoped that an active defense of Donelson would buy the time to allow him to shift from a strategy of dispersed defense to one of concentration. He wanted to strike the invading Federal forces at some point, which in fact occurred several weeks later in the Battle of Shiloh. The sacrifice of Donelson and its garrison was never a part of Johnston's plan.

Before he had even learned of Henry's fall, Johnston began sending men to Donelson. On February 9 Brigadier General Gideon Pillow and 2,000 men arrived at the fort from Clarksville. Pillow exhorted his men to "drive back the ruthless invaders from our soil and again raise the Confederate flag over Fort Henry. . . . Our battle cry, 'Liberty or Death.'" Shortly thereafter Brigadier General Charles Clark came up from Hopkinsville with 2,000 more; Clark's contingent was followed by Brigadier Generals John B. Floyd and Simon Buckner from Russellville with 8,000 additional men.

The Confederate troops were indifferently armed. Their shoulder arms included English-manufactured Enfield rifles, single and double barreled shotguns, hunting rifles, and flint-lock muskets, some of which had been modified with percussion locks.

Johnston's decision to order Floyd to Donelson and place him in command there was, to say the least, unfortunate. For one thing, Floyd did not want to go. Pillow had to leave Donelson and travel to Clarksville to convince him to obey Johnston's order.

Floyd was a prominent Virginian and a former governor of that state. As late as December 1860 he had opposed secession. President James Buchanan had appointed Floyd secre-

GIDEON J. PILLOW

Born in Williamson County, Tennessee, in 1806, Pillow was graduated from the University of Nashville in 1827; he established a law practice at Columbia, Tennessee, and soon became involved in politics; during the 1844 Democratic Convention he worked to secure the presidential nomination for his friend and law partner James K. Polk; following his declaration of war on Mexico, President Polk made Pillow a brigadier general of volunteers; after serving under General Zachary Taylor in northern Mexico, Pillow was promoted to major general and joined general Winfield Scott's drive on Mexico City; Pillow displayed courage but little military skill during the campaign and his personal feud with Scott proved disruptive; supported by Polk and exonerated of misconduct charges brought by Scott, Pillow left the army in 1848 and returned to Tennessee; during the burgeoning sectional crisis of the 1850s, Pillow became a moderate voice, advocating compromise; he twice, in 1852 and 1856, advanced himself as a vice presidential candidate, failing both times to make the Democratic ticket; he supported Stephen Douglas in the 1860 election in hopes of preserving the Union, but with Tennessee's secession in 1861, Pillow offered his services to the state; Governor Isham

Harris appointed him major general and commander of the Provisional Army of Tennessee, but when Tennessee transferred its army to the Confederacy Pillow lost his lofty position and accepted, with much displeasure, the rank of brigadier general, C.S.A; Pillow's Civil War career was hampered by his frequent quarrels with superiors and an inflated opinion of his own military talents; he fought at Belmont, Missouri, in November 1861 and was second-in-command at Fort Donelson in February 1862, when he joined General John B. Floyd in flight, leaving General Simon B. Buckner to surrender the post; relieved of his command pending an investigation, Pillow was eventually restored to duty but with a seriously tarnished reputation; in January 1863 Pillow briefly returned to action, commanding a brigade at Murfreesboro, but he spent most of the remaining war in various administrative assignments. After the war he practiced law in Memphis with Isham Harris, but he suffered serious financial problems that resulted in his bankruptcy in 1877. General Pillow died of yellow fever at Helena, Arkansas, in 1878.

tary of war in 1857, and he served in that post through the end of December 1860. He had been reported in the Northern press as doing much on the eve of secession to scatter the army and shift valuable supplies to military posts in the South. As Grant noted, although Floyd "was a man of talent enough for any civil position, he was no soldier and, probably, did not possess the elements of one."

General Pillow was second in command. A prominent Tennessee lawyer and staunch Democrat, he played a significant role in the 1844 nomination of President James K. Polk, who did so much to bring on war between the United States and Mexico. During that war Polk appointed Pillow a brigadier general of volunteers and later advanced him to major general. Pillow commanded a division in General Winfield Scott's army and engaged in a disruptive quarrel with his commander and

JOHN B. FLOYD

Born in 1806 on his family's estate in Montgomery County, Virginia, Floyd was graduated from South Carolina College in 1829; he practiced law in southwestern Virginia, but soon moved to Arkansas, where he became a cotton planter, but a series of disasters befell him there and almost broke he returned to Virginia; entering politics, he won a seat in the Virginia legislature, and in 1848 was elected governor; he advocated internal improvements, universal suffrage, industrialization, and states rights; upon leaving office he returned to the law, but in 1857 President James Buchanan appointed Floyd secretary of war; Floyd's tenure in the War Department was tainted by several allegations of misconduct, including the mishandling of Indian trust bonds and the shifting of tens of thousands of outdated muskets to Southern arsenals; he also clashed with Mississippi senator and former secretary of war Jefferson Davis over the appointment of Joseph E. Johnston as quartermaster general of the army over Davis' candidate Albert Sidney Johnston—a controversy that would play out during the Civil War; Floyd resigned over Buchanan's decision to main-

even made attempted to supersede him. Grant, who served with Pillow in Mexico, had only contempt for his military abilities. Indeed, a story circulated that Pillow had once ordered his men to pile dirt dug from rifle pits behind them rather than in their front as it should have been. General Lew Wallace described Pillow as a man "of a jealous nature, insubordinate, and quarrelsome."

Brigadier General Buckner was the one capable soldier among the three senior Confederates at Donelson. A native of Kentucky, he had graduated from West Point in 1844. Buckner served with distinction in the Mexican War but left the Army in 1855 to pursue business interests. In 1860 he became head of the Kentucky State Guard. A non-slaveholder, he supported Kentucky neutrality and was offered a brigadier general's commission in the Union army but, after Federal troops moved into

tain Fort Sumter in Charleston Harbor after South Carolina's secession from the Union; although he had opposed secession, when Virginia left the Union he followed suit, and in May 1861 he became a brigadier general in the Confederate service; initially, Floyd served under General Robert E. Lee in western Virginia, but from August to November 1861 he exercised command of the small Army of the Kanawha, campaigning vigorously but unsuccessfully until transferred to Kentucky in December; in February 1862 General Albert S. Johnston ordered Floyd and his Virginia brigade to Fort Donelson, where he assumed command as senior brigadier; with Federal gunboats and the army of U.S. Grant bearing down on the fort, Floyd largely deferred to his second-in-command Gideon Pillow; after a botched breakout attempt, Floyd, Pillow and Simon Buckner opted to surrender, but Floyd feared that his conduct as secretary of war and the charges against him in congress would amount to a death sentence should he surrender; he turned the command over to Pillow, who passed it to Buckner, who ultimately surrendered while Floyd and his Virginians escaped along with Pillow and others; Floyd, who joined Johnston at Nashville and participated in the withdrawal of Confederate forces from middle Tennessee, soon learned that he had been relieved; he then accepted a major general's commission in the Virginia state guard and was serving in southwestern Virginia when his health deteriorated in the summer of 1863; General Floyd died at Abingdon that August.

Kentucky, Buckner accepted a comparable rank in the Confederate service. Floyd arrived at Donelson on the night of February 12 with the last of his command. Polk, meanwhile, sent 1,800 reinforcements from Columbus. By the time Floyd took command, the Donelson garrison had swelled to some 18,000 to 21,000 men in twenty-eight infantry regiments (thirteen from Tennessee, six from Mississippi, four from Virginia, two from Alabama, two from Kentucky, and one from Texas); two independent infantry battalions; one cavalry regiment; and six light artillery batteries.

General Buckner's Division of six regiments and two artillery batteries held the right wing with responsibility for covering land approaches to the water batteries. The left wing and the post garrison fell under the nominal command of Bushrod Johnson, but Pillow had de facto control of these troops. The left wing consisted of six brigades under, from left to right, Colonels Heiman, Thomas J. Davidson, Drake, Gabriel Wharton, John McCausland, and William E. Baldwin, supported by four artillery batteries. The town of Dover became a supply and ordnance depot. The Confederate garrison now braced for attack.

5
THE CAPTURE OF FORT DONELSON

On February 2 Foote had ordered that on the fall of Fort Henry Lieutenant Phelps was to take the three timberclads up the Tennessee River to disable the key Memphis-to-Louisville railroad bridge twenty-five miles above the fort and then raid as far upriver (southward) as the depth of water allowed. Foote himself departed for Cairo with most of his ironclads, leaving the *Carondelet*, behind to support Grant ashore near Henry.

Phelps was held up briefly because drawbridge machinery had been jammed to keep the railroad bridge down, but he landed men and in about an hour they succeeded in opening it. Phelps then left one gunboat behind so that its crew might destroy track while he proceeded upriver.

The sudden arrival of the Federal raiders led the Confederates to burn three steamers filled with ammunition and other supplies. On February 7 at Cerro Gordo, Tennessee, Phelps' gunboats took the 670-ton steamer *Eastport*, which the Confederates had been converting into an ironclad ram. Phelps also seized materials intended for its conversion. Although the *Eastport* had been scuttled, the Federal seamen raised it and returned it to Fort Henry. Later it became a Union ironclad gunboat of the same name, mounting six 11-inch Dahlgren smoothbores and two 100-pounder rifled guns.

On February 8 Phelps captured two small steamers. He and his gunboats got as far south as Florence, Alabama, where they were stopped at Muscle Shoals. There the Confederates set afire three more steamers, although the Federal sailors managed to save a quantity of stores on them marked "Fort Henry."

In informing Halleck of his victory at Fort Henry, Grant said that he expected to take Fort Donelson on the 8th and then return to Fort Henry. This timetable proved overly ambitious. Heavy rain had turned the area roads into quagmires and much of the passage from Henry to Donelson was in fact under water, making the movement of artillery and baggage trains all but impossible. Then too, the gunboats were still away. On the 8th Grant telegraphed Halleck, "I contemplated taking Fort Donelson to-day with infantry and cavalry alone, but all my troops may be kept busily engaged in saving what we now have from the rapidly rising water."

On the 7th Grant had taken his staff and part of a cavalry regiment to conduct a reconnaissance in force to within about a mile of Donelson's outer works. He wrote in his *Memoirs* that at the time he remarked to his staff that, "I had known General Pillow in Mexico, and judged that with any force, no matter how small, I could march up to within gunshot of any entrenchments he was given to hold." Grant also observed, "I knew that Floyd was in command, but he was no soldier, and I judged that he would yield to Pillow's pretensions." As expected there was no Confederate opposition to the reconnaissance, which discovered that there were two roads available for moving troops. These diverged but came together about two and a half miles before Dover.

Foote, meanwhile, put together his riverine assault force. Grant urged Foote to order the gunboats left at Cairo to proceed up the Cumberland without waiting for those that had gone to Eastport and Florence. As it worked out the *Tyler* (Lieutenant William Gwin) and *Conestoga* (Lieutenant Phelps) returned from their raid up the Tennessee and were available, as was the *Carondelet* (Commander Walke). The latter had returned to Fort Henry on the 10th and Grant requested that Walke use it and the timberclads to secure control of the Cumberland as close to Donelson as possible. The *Carondelet* arrived off that fort on February 12.

The *Essex* and *Cincinnati* could not be made ready in time. Some thirty seamen had deserted, but Foote managed to find replacements and left with the *St. Louis* (Lieutenant Paulding), *Louisville* (Commander Benjamin Dove), and *Pittsburg* (Lieutenant Egbert Thompson). Although he felt that his squadron was not ready, Foote sailed on Grant's urging. With a much longer run to the destination, Foote's gunboats did not arrive in the vicinity of Fort Donelson until the night of the 13th, only to find that Grant's troops had already invested Donelson. Many of the officers and men on the flotilla believed they could replicate their easy victory at Fort Henry, but for both the Army and Navy Donelson would be quite different.

Halleck was singularly noncommittal on the matter of Grant's plans to attack Donelson. Grant later wrote that "General Halleck did not approve or disapprove of my going to Fort Donelson. He said nothing whatever to me on the subject." Halleck did, however, order Grant to reinforce Henry strongly, a directive that reached Grant when he was already at Donelson. And Halleck did work to get as many reinforcements to the point of battle as possible. As he put it, "We have stirring times in Kentucky and Tennessee, and want every man we can get." General David Hunter sent men from Kansas and Buell, too late, sent General Nelson's large division. The War Department also ordered scattered fragments of companies in the West consolidated into regiments to be sent to Donelson. Many of these men were virtually untrained and would have to learn on the job. Grant was convinced that the Confederates would move quickly to reinforce Donelson and he was anxious to attack as soon as possible. As he put it, "I felt that 15,000 men on the 8th would be more effective than 50,000 a month later."

JOHN A. McCLERNAND

Born Kentucky 1812; as a child, McClernand moved with his family to Illinois; he studied law and was admitted to the bar in 1832, but other interests kept him from practicing; he fought in the Black Hawk War and edited a newspaper before entering the state assembly in 1836, serving until 1843, when he took a seat in the U.S. House of Representatives as a Democrat; a fine orator, he served a total of five terms in the House (1843-1851 and 1859-1861), taking an active part in the Compromise of 1850; although he possessed a fierce dislike for abolitionists, he was nonetheless unwavering in his support of the Union; with the onset of the Civil War, McClernand's efforts to rally support and recruit troops for the Federal army proved invaluable; recognizing McClernand's political value, President Lincoln appointed him brigadier general of U.S. Volunteers in August 1861; that October he resigned his seat in Congress to command a brigade in Missouri and southern Illinois, participating in the Battle of Belmont; in February 1862 McClernand took command of a division in the Army of the Tennessee, and was promoted to major general of Volunteers in March; he saw action at Fort Donelson, Shiloh, and Corinth, leav-

On the night of February 11 Grant, still at Henry, moved McClernand's Division a few miles east toward Donelson to more solid ground in order to clear the road as much as possible. On the 12th, just as the advance began, the first Union reinforcements arrived—Colonel John M. Thayer's Brigade of two full regiments. Grant ordered Thayer to reverse direction without debarking and follow the gunboats from Henry down the Tennessee, up the Ohio, and then up the Cumberland.

Also on the 12th Grant started out by land for Donelson with McClernand's (First) Division and Smith's (Second) Division. He brought along eight artillery batteries (3.67-inch,

ing the army in October to recruit a new army, which he would command in a move against Vicksburg; he successfully raised a large force, which he then forwarded to Memphis, only to have it commandeered by General W.T. Sherman for his failed attack on Chickasaw Bayou; McClernand then took command and led his short-lived Army of the Mississippi in a successful attack on Arkansas Post; shortly thereafter, his command was absorbed into General U.S. Grant's Army of the Tennessee, part of it as the Thirteenth Corps, with McClernand as commander; during the Vicksburg Campaign, McClernand angered his superiors by releasing stories to newspapers that praised the efforts of his command at the expense of the rest of the army; although he performed reasonably well in the campaign, he was relieved in June, and did not return to duty until 1864, when he again headed the Thirteenth Corps in the Department of the Gulf during the Red River Campaign; suffering from malaria, he resigned in November 1864; after the war he served as a circuit judge from 1870 to 1873 and was active in Democratic politics, chairing the party's national convention in 1876; he died at Springfield, Illinois, in 1900. Despite his self-congratulatory reports and adversarial relationships with Grant and others, McClernand made important contributions to the Union war effort, especially as a recruiter. As a combat commander, he showed certain ability, but his impact on the army in the field was largely negative. Like other political appointees, he carried from the war a deep resentment of West Point-educated professional soldiers.

20-pounder, Parrott rifled guns and 24-pounder howitzers) and part of a cavalry regiment. In all he commanded 15,000 men in twenty-five regiments.

The weather had turned unseasonably warm. As General Lew Wallace observed, the 12th was "a day of summer. River, land, and sky fairly shimmered with warmth." Many of the men chose to leave behind knapsacks, heavy overcoats, and blankets, or they cast them aside en route, something they would soon have cause to regret.

The Federal troops met no resistance before running into Confederate pickets west of Fort Donelson. Grant set up his headquarters in a small log house on the Dover road about two miles west of town. He ordered Smith to take up a position on the left facing Buckner's Confederate right wing and McClernand to oppose the Confederate left wing under Pillow. For two days, February 12 and 13, 15,000 unentrenched Federal troops confronted perhaps 21,000 entrenched Confederates but, fortunately for Grant, Floyd made no effort to dislodge him.

Before dawn on the 13th Federal sharpshooters left camp and were soon busy sniping at Confederate soldiers working to improve the forward defenses. Additional firing occurred as Grant's skirmishers established the Confederate lines. As the sun came up Federal regiments extended their lines north and south to make the investment as complete as possible. Artillery horses hauled guns and caissons down hollows and up hills as gunners moved their batteries into position. Then, one battery after another on both sides opened fire as "the regiments marched, route-step, colors flying, after their colonels."

When McClernand arrived at his appointed location and began to place his brigades he discovered that the Confederate line was too long for him to envelop. To extend his force to the end of the Confederate left would leave his own line dangerously thin and without reserves. Moreover, near the extremity of the Rebel left was the Charlotte road, a resupply route and possible escape hatch to Nashville that had to be closed. On learning of this Grant ordered up Lew Wallace's Brigade of Smith's Division, which he had left behind at Fort Henry. Wallace's 2,500 men, two infantry regiments and an artillery battery, would arrive at Donelson at noon on the 14th.

Smith's two remaining brigades held the Federal left to Hickman's Creek. The attackers did not entrench but their line generally followed the crest of ridges and the troops could take position a bit back from the crests and be as protected as if they had dug rifle pits.

Up to this point Federal troops had initiated the fighting. As Grant recalled, there was no conflict "further than what we brought on by ourselves. Only one gunboat had arrived. There was a little skirmishing each day, brought on by the movement of our troops in securing commanding positions."

The gunboat was the *Carondelet*. Towed by the steamer *Alps*, it arrived near Donelson at 11:30 AM on the 12th. Not sighting any Union troops ashore, Commander Walke ordered about ten rounds fired at Fort Donelson from long range "to unmask the silent enemy, and to announce my arrival to General Grant." There was no Confederate reply. The gunboat then dropped downriver a few miles and anchored for the night. The next morning the gunboat returned to near Donelson, where Walke received a message from Grant asking him to make another demonstration at 10:00 AM to divert the Confederates while his troops improved their own lines.

The *Carondelet* then got under way and, masked by a heavily wooded point on the river bank, fired 139 70-pound and 64-pound shells at the Confederate positions from long range. This time the Confederates returned fire. Most of their shots passed high but two hit home. At 11:30 one of these, a 128-pound solid shot from their rifled gun in the upper battery, burst through the front casemate, wounding a half dozen members of the crew, and doing slight damage to the ship's machinery. The *Carondelet* halted fire briefly to transfer wounded to the *Alps* and then lobbed another forty-five shells into the fort. Federal gunners ceased fire only after expending almost all of their ammunition.

In the exchange one of the *Carondelet's* shots struck a Confederate 32-pounder, disabling it and killing two men, including Captain Joseph Dixon, an engineer who had assisted Lieutenant Colonel Gilmer in the construction of both Henry and Donelson. Five other Rebels were wounded. According to some Confederate defenders the effects from the *Carondelet's* shelling on the 13th were greater than that of the next day from the entire Federal squadron.

Thus far there had been no major fighting between the two armies; firing had been limited largely to skirmishing, sniping, and artillery exchanges. That changed shortly after noon on the 13th when, despite Grant's order not to bring on a general engagement, McClernand attempted to capture Captain Frank Maney's battery of Colonel Heiman's Brigade. Located in the center of the Confederate line, the battery had been annoying the Illinois general's men. McClernand, therefore, sent three regiments to assault a position that was supported by the bulk of Confederate strength.

Predictably, the assault failed, although the troops tried three times and the commander of the Third Brigade, Colonel William R. Morrison, was badly wounded while leading his men. During the last charge dead leaves ignited and the ensuing fire killed a number of wounded on both sides. Although Union artillery fire produced some Confederate casualties, losses were far heavier among the attackers (158 killed and wounded).

Grant was displeased that the attack had been attempted. He wrote laconically in his *Memoirs*, "the loss on our side was great for the number of men engaged." But as Federal participant Lieutenant Colonel (later Brevet Major General) Manning F. Force noted, "the pertinacity of the attack through the day prevented the besieged from suspecting the inferiority in numbers of the attacking force."

That afternoon the weather changed dramatically from impending spring back to winter, and a fierce wind brought sleet and snow. With the temperature plummeting to only twelve degrees, there was much suffering on both sides. Frostbite became a major concern.

At 11:30 on the night of the 13th Commodore Foote arrived with the ironclads *St. Louis* (flagship), *Louisville*, and *Pittsburg*. Behind them the *Tyler* and *Conestoga* convoyed transports carrying Thayer's Brigade. Thayer's men came ashore the next morning and Wallace's Brigade arrived at noon from Fort Henry. Grant then restored Wallace's Brigade to Smith's Division and gave Wallace command of what became known as the Third Division, composed of Thayer's Brigade of Ohio and Nebraska troops and two other brigades of reinforcements from Kentucky, Indiana, and Illinois that had arrived with Foote. This new division now took over the center between Smith's and McClernand's Divisions. Wallace opposed Confederate brigades under Colonels Heiman, Drake, and Davidson.

The Confederates were now completely invested, except along the Cumberland River above Dover. Floyd had wasted a splendid opportunity. If his troops had attacked on the 13th they could have pushed Grant back to Fort Henry and, as Wallace noted, "more than offset Foote's conquest." After the 14th that was no longer possible.

Grant used the 14th to shift units and set boundary lines. Skirmishers exchanged shots and artillery units ranged their guns, but the day was relatively quiet as far as actual fighting on land was concerned. McClernand extended his right flank closer to the Cumberland and posted some of his units across three roads off Wynn's Ferry Road, the main ridge road that ran across the hollow through the Confederate entrenchments into Dover. Federal cavalry also reconnoitered the extreme

LEW WALLACE

Born at Brookville, Indiana, in 1827, the son of a future Indiana governor, Lewis "Lew" Wallace had a taste for adventure but little interest in studies; he worked as a clerk and as a newspaper reporter before serving as a volunteer officer during the Mexican War; after the war he passed the Indiana bar and established a law practice; elected to the state senate in 1856, Wallace was active in the Montgomery County militia; with the outbreak of the Civil War, he was appointed adjutant general of Indiana, responsible for raising regiments for Federal service; but in late April 1861 Wallace was appointed colonel of the 11th Indiana Infantry, which he led to western Virginia; after a successful engagement at Romney, Wallace was promoted to brigadier general of U.S. Volunteers and ordered to the Western Theater, where in February 1862 he commanded a division under General U.S. Grant at Fort Donelson; promoted to major general of volunteers in March 1862, he led a division in the Battle of Shiloh, but his performance during that battle drew much criticism and he was eventually relieved of command; he spent much of the next two years in various administrative assignments, but in March 1864 he assumed command of the Middle Department and the Eighth Army Corps with headquarters at Baltimore; during Confederate General Jubal Early's drive on Washington in July 1864, Wallace led a small force in an attempt to block Early's advance at Monocacy Junction, Maryland; although driven from the field by a superior force, Wallace's command bought valuable time to prepare Washington for attack; after the war he participated in the trial of the Lincoln assassination conspirators and was president of the court-martial that convicted Andersonville Prison commandant Henry Wirz. Resigning from the service in November 1865, Wallace supported the efforts to oust Emperor Maximilian in Mexico; in 1878 he was appointed governor of the turbulent New Mexico Territory, working to resolve the Lincoln County War and to bring outlaw Billy the Kid to justice; during his time at Santa Fe, Wallace wrote *Ben Hur: A Tale of the Christ,* a literary classic that brought the author lasting fame; in 1881 he was named minister to Turkey, serving there until 1885; General Wallace died at Crawfordsville, Indiana, in 1905.

enemy left flank to the overflowed creek bottom from the Cumberland just upriver from Dover.

On the morning of the 14th senior Confederate commanders met and decided to attempt a breakout before increasing Federal reinforcements made it impossible. Their plan called for Pillow's forces to lead an attack against the Federal right flank with Buckner's forces covering the rear if it was then decided to retreat to Nashville by way of Charlotte. Buckner made the necessary dispositions for his men, but early that afternoon Floyd countermanded the order on the insistence of General Pillow, who had drawn out his troops but then thought it too late for an attempt that day.

Grant, meanwhile, had called on Foote for a naval attack. Grant's plan was to hold the Confederates within the fort while the Foote's flotilla attacked at close quarters and reduced the water batteries. If possible, some of the gunboats were to run past the batteries and get south of Dover to cut off Confederate resupply from the river.

Although Foote would have preferred a delay until he could make a personal reconnaissance, he complied with Grant's request. That morning gunboat crews placed hard materials, such as chains, lumber, and bags of coal on the upper decks of the gunboats to try to protect them from plunging shot. Foote was ready by the afternoon and the assault began shortly before 3:00, with the same formation as at Fort Henry—the *St. Louis* (flagship), *Carondelet, Louisville,* and *Pittsburg* in front. The vulnerable timberclads *Tyler* and *Conestoga* followed about a thousand yards to the rear, beyond the range of Donelson's guns.

Surprise was impossible; the Confederates had an excellent field of fire up a long, straight stretch of the Cumberland, while at the same time their earthen works were difficult to locate from the water. At about 3:30 PM and at 1,500-yards range the Confederates fired two shots from their 10-inch Columbiad against the advancing ships. Both rounds fell short.

Shortly thereafter the *St. Louis* opened fire and the other gunboats followed suit. Foote changed speed from time to time to try to reduce the accuracy of the Confederate fire. The Union ships fired rapidly until they were within 400 yards of the battery. They may have been closer than that. Grant, observing the fight from the shore, estimated that the *Carondelet* came to within two hundred yards of the water battery.

The firing continued for an hour and a half. The Confederates found the height of their water battery and guns on the bluff to be a great advantage; their elevation permitted plunging fire that nullified the sloping Union armor by hitting it at right angles. This soon began to tell. As Walke described it, the shot "knocked the plating to pieces, and sent fragments of iron and splinters into the pilots, one of whom fell mortally wounded, and was taken below . . . and still they came, harder and faster, taking flag-staffs and smoke-stacks, and tearing off their side armor as lightning tears the bark from a tree."

The nearness of the attacking fleet aided the inexperienced Confederate gunners by allowing them to bring more of their guns into action and to fire more accurately. The gunboats, meanwhile, could use only their three bow guns and the gunners found it difficult to locate the Confederate positions and to elevate their guns sufficiently to bring their enemy under fire.

The steering mechanisms of two on the warships were soon shot away and pilot houses of two others were badly damaged. The flagship *St. Louis* alone was hit fifty-nine times and Foote was wounded in the left arm and left foot by splinters from a shell that killed the pilot standing next to him and took away the ship's wheel. The *Louisville*, disabled by a shot that carried away its rudder chains, drifted out of action. Aboard the *Carondelet* a rifled gun, loaded too hastily, blew up on firing and wounded more than a dozen men. Two Confederate hits killed four men. More would have been casualties had not lookouts shouted warnings of incoming Confederate shot to allow the men time to duck. Still, Walke reported that there

Gunboat Attack on Fort Donelson

was so much blood on the decks "that our men could not work the guns without slipping."

The *Carondelet*, which took fifty-four hits, sustained the most damage. The *Pittsburg*, also in difficulty, crashed into the *Carondelet* and broke its rudder. The *St. Louis* was disabled by the *Tyler*, when the latter smashed into her steering gear. Three of the four ironclads were now *hors d'combat*, drifting downstream. In the flotilla as a whole eleven men were killed and forty-three wounded, half of these on the *Carondelet*. Incredibly, there were no casualties among the defenders, nor any damage to the battery or its armament.

Confederate soldiers broke into cheers as the Union vessels withdrew. The engagement had the opposite effect on the Federals, although damage to the gunboats was not as severe as it seemed at first—none sustained serious injury.

Foote himself said he had taken his ships in against Donelson at the "urgent request of General Halleck and General Grant, who regarded the movement as a military necessity, although not in my opinion properly prepared." He telegraphed his wife, "I will not go so near again, although at Fort Henry I produced an effect by it. We ought to have been victorious at Donelson, as we fought harder than at Henry. I went into it against my judgment by order of Halleck." He gave a different assessment in his official report: "We had every reason to believe that in fifteen minutes more, could the action have been continued, it would have resulted in the capture of the forts." Foote based this on the fact that Rebel fire had slackened and "he was running from his batteries" when the *St. Louis* and *Louisville* were forced to retire. There was little evidence to support this optimistic assessment.

Confederate Colonel Nathan Bedford Forrest, watching from land, described the duel in these words:

> Of the attack I was an eyewitness, and have never seen a description which did anything like justice to the attack or defense. More determination could not have been exhibited by the attacking party, while more coolness and bravery never was manifested than was seen in our artillerists. Never was there greater anxiety depicted in the faces of brave men than during the terrific roar of cannon, relieved ever and anon by the slow but regular report of our one single 10-inch gun. Never were there men more jubilant than when the victory crowned the steady bravery of our little fort; old men wept; shout upon shout went up; the gunboats driven back; the army was in the best possible spirits, feeling that, relieved of their greatest terror, they could whip any land force that could be brought against them.

Writing with the benefit of hindsight, Admiral David Porter thought that Foote might have sent his remaining gunboats past the fort that night and then taken Donelson under fire the next day from the more advantageous upriver approach. This would have had the added advantage of cutting off the Confederate garrison from escape across or up the river by boat.

With their repulse of the land attack on the 13th, the Confederates had their second success. River communication with Nashville remained open. As General Lew Wallace noted, this buoyed the Confederates: "The winds that blew sleet and snow over Donelson that night were not so unendurable as they might have been."

Federal reinforcements continued to arrive, however. Toward evening on the 14th Grant ordered Colonel John McArthur to have his men occupy ground on the extreme right of the line as a reserve to troops under Colonel Richard Oglesby. McArthur's men reached the assigned position in the dark and "encamped for the night, without instructions and without adequate knowledge of the nature of the ground in front and on the right." The troops had no shelter and the night was again very cold with wind, snow, and sleet. The weather greatly complicated the lives of both the defenders and attackers but especially affected the Federals. Many defenders had huts for protection, while the besiegers lacked even tents. Men at the front lines on both sides could not light fires for fear of giving away their positions. Grant went to sleep on the night of the 14th without knowing whether he would have to settle in for a long siege, order up tents, or instruct the men to build huts.

At 2:00 AM on the 15th a message arrived at Grant's head-quarters from Foote requesting a meeting. Foote wrote that his wounds prevented him from traveling and requested that the two meet aboard his flagship four miles downstream. Grant then left for the meeting but not before informing his three division commanders of his absence. He instructed them to hold their positions and not to initiate any engagement unless they received express orders from him. Later Grant was criticized for not designating a commander to act in his absence.

Weather conditions slowed Grant's trip to Foote. When he reached the shore near the *St. Louis*, a small boat took him out to the flagship. There Foote briefed Grant on the damage to the squadron and suggested that the troops ashore entrench while he returned with the two most seriously damaged gun-boats to Mound City and effected repairs. He would leave the other two ironclads behind to protect the transports at the landing. Foote told Grant that he believed he could return in ten days, he hoped with the powerful *Benton* and mortar boats, at which time they could renew the attack. When the two men parted it was on the understanding that they would follow Foote's plan, but, as Grant put it later, "the enemy relieved me from that necessity."

When he went to meet with Foote, Grant assumed that any new fighting at Donelson would be initiated by him, which was one reason why he did not designate someone to act in his absence. (As Shelby Foote notes, this reflected a pattern in Grant's generalship: "he always thought more about what he planned to do to the enemy than what his enemy might do to him.") Grant based this assumption on the fact that this had been true thus far and that his army had greatly increased its strength. During the first two days of the investment Grant had only 15,000 men and no gunboats. Now he had six warships, Wallace's new division, and the 2,500 men from Fort Henry.

The Confederate commanders were not willing to wait, however. Although encouraged by their repulse of the Union squadron, they knew that their position was untenable. Grant was increasing his strength steadily and tightening the noose. The Union right flank now extended almost to Lick Creek, apparently completing the land encirclement. On the night of the 14th, therefore, Generals Floyd, Pillow, and Buckner met at the Dover Hotel to consider their options.

The Confederate commanders reached the same conclusion of their earlier meeting. Pillow's Division, assisted by cavalry, would attack along the west bank of the Cumberland River against McClernand's Division on the right flank. Pillow's job was to open up an escape route, rolling up Federal troops on his front and pushing them west. Buckner's men would then sortie and strike the center of McClernand's Division. When the Federal right flank had been rolled back into the center, Pillow would lead the retreat to Charlotte. Buckner would hold the Union center at bay outside the entrenchments until the remainder of the Confederate garrison had escaped and then serve as the army's rear guard during the retreat.

But Confederate planning was haphazard. Although General Bushrod Johnson and the various brigade commanders were informed of the plan, no instructions were issued as to what the men were to carry and some regiments packed neither knapsacks nor rations.

Pillow's Division assembled that night. The men left their rifle pits as quietly as possible and, as on the previous day, gathered to the rear of the extreme left of the line. The Confederates were able to accomplish this without alarming Federal pickets, although no doubt the howling wind played a part.

The Confederate attack began at 6:00 on the morning of the 15th, just as Federal buglers sounded reveille. It caught Colonel Oglesby's Brigade of McClernand's Division completely by surprise. In a hard-fought close action the Federal troops, ammunition exhausted, were driven back, although in good order—the men holding up their empty cartridge cases to show they were not cowards. The brigade suffered 836 casualties. As Pillow's men deployed en echelon they came into contact with Colonel W.H.L. Wallace's Brigade to Oglesby's left. The Federal right wing was being rolled up and giving way.

Buckner's Division was still within the entrenchments. As he recalled, "In view of the heavy duty which I expected my division to undergo in covering the retreat of the army, I thought it unadvisable to attempt an assault at this time in my front until the enemy's batteries were to some extent crippled and their supports shaken by the fire of my artillery." At about 9:00, however, Pillow ordered Buckner to advance. Buckner then sent three regiments forward against McClernand's left, supported by three batteries. The brunt of this assault fell on W.H.L. Wallace's Brigade. For a time Wallace withstood attacks from both Buckner's men and Pillow's Division. As Lew Wallace described it,

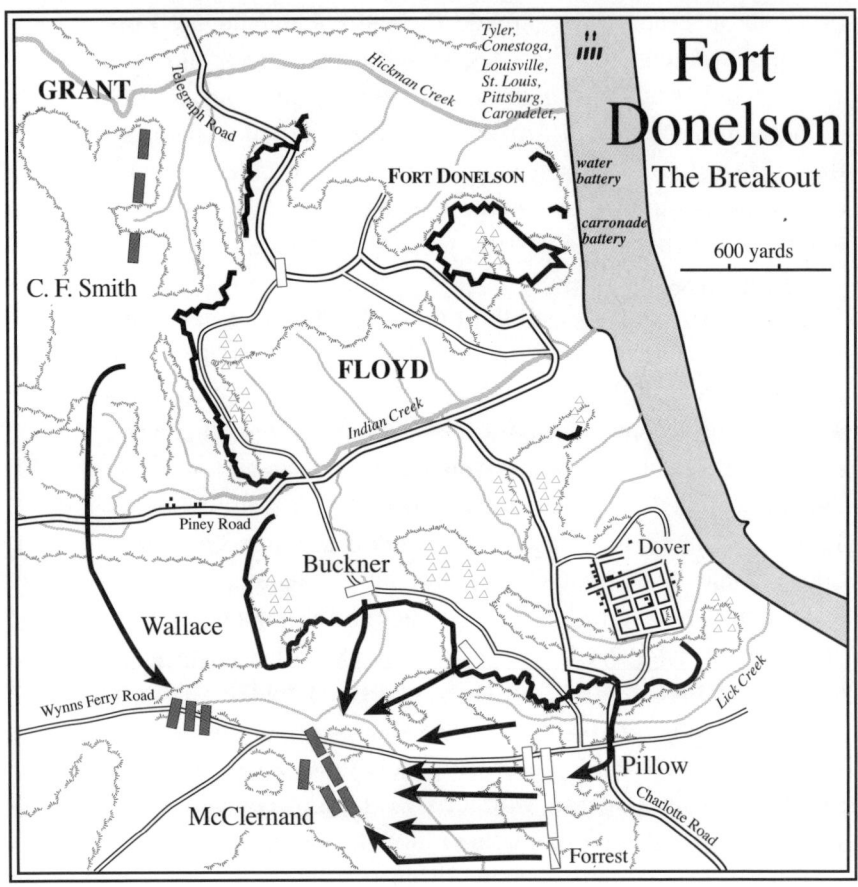

GRANT

C. F. Smith

Telegraph Road

Hickman Creek

Tyler,
Conestoga,
Louisville,
St. Louis,
Pittsburg,
Carondelet,

Fort Donelson

water battery

carronade battery

Fort Donelson

The Breakout

600 yards

FLOYD

Indian Creek

Piney Road

Buckner

Wallace

Wynns Ferry Road

McClernand

Dover

Lick Creek

Pillow

Charlotte Road

Forrest

The roar never slackened. Men fell by the score, reddening the snow with their blood. The smoke, in pallid white clouds, clung to the underbrush and tree-tops as if to screen the combatants from each other. Close to the ground the flame of musketry and cannon tinted everything a lurid red.

W.H.L. Wallace's two Federal batteries soon expended their ammunition, in one case 1,700 rounds for a battery of six guns, or an average of 384 rounds per gun. The infantrymen also had fired their last cartridges, leaving Colonel Wallace little option but to retire. One battery had only two horses left and could save only one of its three guns. The brigade retreated a half mile.

At the same time Confederate cavalry under Forrest attacked the Federal right. By 11:00 Pillow held the road to Charlotte and the entire area that had been occupied by McClernand's Division. He sent an aide to the nearest telegraph station with a dispatch for General Johnston: "On the honor of a soldier, the day is ours!" With the escape route open all that remained was for Pillow to deploy his regiments in column and begin the march to safety. Disagreement and confusion among their generals now cost the Confederates that chance.

Imagining that he was now in position to defeat Grant and force the Federals back to Henry and to their transports on the Cumberland, Pillow ignored Floyd's orders and continued the attack. This decision threw away the only chance for the Donelson garrison to escape and in fact hastened its surrender. Pillow ordered Buckner to throw his regiments at Union forces across a gorge. The whole Confederate army save a few detachments left in the fort was now pushing McClernand's Division southwest. Pillow's Division, with Forrest's cavalry on its left flank, advanced south of Wynn's Ferry Road, moving parallel to the line of entrenchments and to the southwest, while Buckner's men moved astride and north of the road.

General Lew Wallace, mindful of Grant's command not to move without an express order from him, had refused McClernand's first appeal for assistance but sent an officer to Grant's headquarters for instructions. Grant's staff was unwilling to act in his absence but with Oglesby's flank now turned and the situation desperate, Wallace acted on his own and ordered Colonel Charles Cruft's Brigade forward. It was soon heavily engaged, but, unsupported, it too was forced to retreat.

Lew Wallace, in the rear with his single remaining brigade commanded by Colonel John A. Thayer, was conferring with Grant's aide Captain John A. Rawlins when he heard a great commotion. Wallace sent an orderly to determine the cause. The aide returned with news that Oglesby's and W. H. L. Wallace's Brigades were retreating along Wynn's Ferry Road.

At that point an officer rode past General Wallace and shouted, "All's lost! Save yourselves!" Wallace then ordered Thayer's Brigade forward at double-quick. The men passed by the two retreating brigades and deployed just before a gorge. One battery also arrived and had barely unlimbered before the Confederates struck.

Savage fighting erupted. As Lew Wallace described it, "The woods rang with musketry and artillery. The brush on the slope of the hill was mowed away with bullets. A great cloud arose and shut out the woods and the narrow valley below." After some ten minutes deliberate aimed fire by Thayer's Brigade repulsed the attackers, who then fell back in the direction of their entrenchments. Cruft's Brigade formed up to the right of Thayer's, and Colonels Wallace and Oglesby reformed their brigades behind Thayer, secured ammunition, and awaited orders. The Confederate advance had been halted.

Pillow then threw away the opportunity gained. As he later explained, he thought the plan all along had been to return to the fort, gather rations, retrieve the artillery and supply wagons, and then leave. Pillow ordered Buckner to return to the entrenchments. Surprised, Buckner was on the point of carrying out the order when Floyd came up. The two generals agreed that the original escape plan should be followed and Floyd ordered Buckner to stay in place until he could meet with Pillow. Pillow then easily convinced Floyd, who ordered Buckner to return to the fort and immediately take up his former position on the now-vulnerable Confederate right. Later Pillow sought unsuccessfully to shift the blame to Buckner by claiming that "the necessity for the surrender was caused by

General Buckner's unsuccessful attack on the Wynn's Ferry road battery and his failure to hold his rifle pits."

Grant now intervened. When he had stepped ashore after leaving the *St. Louis*, he had been met by his shaken aide Captain William Hillyer, who had ridden to the landing to inform him of the desperate situation. Grant then rode to the battle as fast as his horse could travel on the icy roads and reached General Wallace's command post at about 1:00 PM. He rode up while Wallace and McClernand were in conversation. He recalled later that he was upset to find "men standing in knots talking in the most excited manner. No officer seemed to be giving any directions."

Wallace remembered Grant as "wholly unexcited." Grant then ordered the troops to entrench; reinforcements were en route, he said, and they should wait for their arrival. On being told that the road to Charlotte lay open, Grant then changed his mind and announced in "his ordinary quiet voice" to McClernand and Wallace, "Gentlemen, the position on the right must be retaken." With that he galloped off. Wallace watched Grant ride away, "wondering at the simplicity of the words in a matter involving so much."

In his *Memoirs* Grant made no mention of Wallace having pointed out the possibility of a Confederate escape, indeed he did not even refer to a conversation with his two generals. He simply wrote, "I heard some of the men say that the enemy had come out with knapsacks, and haversacks filled with rations." This convinced him that the Confederates were attempting to break out. He also recalled the order he had given to bring demoralized soldiers back into the line: "I directed Colonel [Joseph] Webster to ride with me and call out to the men as we passed: 'Fill your cartridge-boxes, quick, and get into line; the enemy is trying to escape and he must not be permitted to do so.' This acted like a charm. The men wanted some one to give them a command."

Grant reasoned that in order to break through on his right

the Confederates must have weakened their lines elsewhere. On the way to the fighting he had passed through the Federal left and center, both of which he judged in excellent shape. If General Smith could mount an immediate attack against the Confederate right wing before the Confederates could redistribute their forces it might change the whole course of the battle. Grant told an aide, "The one who attacks first now will be victorious." He then added, "The enemy will have to be in a hurry to get ahead of me."

Smith needed no urging. Grant noted, "the general was off in an incredibly short time." At 2:00 PM Smith ordered an attack by Colonel J.G. Lauman's Brigade, reinforced with an additional regiment and deployed in battalion columns of five companies each. Sharpshooters on the flanks provided protection as the battalions moved forward without firing until they had worked their way through the abatis. Disregarding Rebel fire the men moved up the slope toward the Confederate entrenchments. Smith, on horseback and in the front rank, encouraged his men forward by word and example as Confederates abandoned their rifle pits. One report has Smith shouting, "Come on you volunteers, come on. This is your chance. You volunteered to be killed for love of country and now you can be!"

Federal troops using the bayonet soon reached the breastworks, climbed over them, and formed into line to drive the defending Confederates back. At this point Buckner's men arrived. Although they halted the advance, they were unable to force the invaders out of the works. Smith then called up artillery. Two 2.9-inch (10-pounder) Parrott guns arrived and were positioned within the fort, where Smith had his men entrench for the night and stayed with them without shelter. Smith's attack had cost 61 Union dead and 157 wounded, but the ground taken was as high as any in the fort and its capture placed the entire Confederate position in jeopardy.

As General Smith's forces moved out on the left flank,

CHARLES F. SMITH

Born at Philadelphia in 1807, Smith was graduated from the U.S. Military Academy in 1825, nineteenth in his class of thirty-seven; posted to the 2d Artillery, he served on garrison duty before becoming an instructor at West Point; he remained at his alma mater for thirteen years, becoming commandant of cadets; many future Civil War generals passed through the academy during Smith's time there, including William T. Sherman and U.S. Grant, who would become his commander during the Henry-Donelson Campaign of 1862. During the Mexican War, Smith saw much action, serving with General Zachary Taylor in the north and with General Winfield Scott in the drive on Mexico City; he earned three brevets for gallantry; Smith had risen through the ranks to lieutenant colonel of the 10th Infantry, when he participated in the 1858 Mormon Expedition, after which he remained as commander of the Department of Utah. Ordered to Washington following the outbreak of the Civil War, Smith briefly took charge of troops in the capital city; he then rendered valuable recruiting services before moving to the Western Theater to assume command of the District of Western Kentucky; promoted to brigadier general of U.S. Volunteers in August 1861 (he received the regular rank of colonel the following month), Smith was active in securing the important area around Paducah; he led a division under his former student Grant in the February 1862 advance on Fort Henry and won high praise for his actions in compelling the surrender of Fort Donelson; promoted to major general of volunteers, he replaced Grant as commander of what became the Army of the Tennessee; having moved the army to Pittsburg Landing on the Tennessee  River in March, Smith cut a leg jumping into a boat; the wound became infected and forced Smith to relinquish command to Grant before the Battle of Shiloh; taken to nearby Savannah, Tennessee, to recover, Smith grew weaker as the infection intensified. General Smith, regarded by some the best officer in the Union, died from complications at Grant's headquarters on April 25, 1862.

General Wallace's Third Division advanced on the right to retake the ground lost earlier. Colonel M. L. Smith's Brigade moved by bounds. Smith had his men lie prone and fire from that position. As soon as Confederate return fire slackened, he ordered his regiments to rise up, charge, and then lie prone again before return fire could do much damage. By 3:30 in the afternoon the Confederates were again within the fort. Although they retired in good order and took with them six Union guns, several thousand small arms, and at least two hundred prisoners, they were both disappointed and discouraged.

Five Federal infantry regiments reached the Donelson area on river transport on the evening of the 15th. Union strength was now up to 27,000 men. Although Grant had no artillery except the eight batteries brought with him from Fort Henry, it was no longer possible for the bulk of the Confederates to escape. Grant now urged Foote to return the gunboats and lend moral support. The *St. Louis* and *Louisville* did reappear and lobbed a few shells into the fort, although this demonstration proved unnecessary.

That night Generals Floyd, Pillow, and Buckner met at the Dover Hotel to assess the situation, the meeting continuing into the early hours of the 16th. It began with some recrimination between Buckner and Pillow over the plan to be executed. The generals then agreed to attempt a retreat early the next morning over the ground Pillow had gained previously—but only if the Federals had not reoccupied it in strength. They asked Colonel Forrest to send out scouts to determine the condition of the road running next to the river and to report the presence of Federal troops there. The scouts returned with word that they had seen no enemy troops but there were fires burning in the same places as the night before. They also reported that about one hundred yards of road was under some three feet of water. They thought infantry could not pass through it but that cavalry might.

Pillow then proposed that they attempt to cut their way out,

Buckner said that was no longer possible. He was prepared to fight on only if, as he understood it, the object of defending Donelson was to cover Johnston's retreat to Nashville. Floyd announced that Johnston's troops had already reached Nashville, at which Buckner advocated surrender. He pointed out that the Federal troops who had taken a portion of the Confederate right would almost certainly attack at first light and his men would not be able to hold for half an hour.

Besides that the men were in no condition to march. Buckner detailed his position in his official report:

> Both officers [Floyd and Pillow] have correctly stated that I regarded the position of the army as desperate, and that an attempt to extricate it by another battle, in the suffering and exhausted condition of the troops, was almost hopeless. The troops had been worn down with watching, with labor, with fighting. Many of them were frosted by the intensity of the cold; all of them were suffering and exhausted by their incessant labors. There had been no regular issue of rations for a number of days and scarcely any means of cooking. Their ammunition was nearly expended. We were completely invested by a force fully four times the strength of our own. In their exhausted condition they could not have made a march.

Pillow then stated: "Gentlemen, if we cannot cut our way out nor fight on there is no alternative left us but capitulation, and I am determined that I will never surrender the command nor will I ever surrender myself a prisoner. I will die first." Floyd shared Pillow's determination for personal reasons. As one of the highest ranking former U.S. government officials to rally to the Confederacy, he believed that the betrayal of his oath of loyalty to the Constitution would lead to his trial for treason if captured. In his *Memoirs* Grant concurred with this assessment and, indeed, Floyd was at the time under indictment by a grand jury in Washington, D.C., for malversation as secretary of war and for complicity in embezzlement of public funds.

Pillow remarked that he thought there were no two people in the Confederacy whom the Yankees would prefer to capture than himself and Floyd. Pillow then asked Floyd about the propriety of accompanying him. Floyd answered "that it was a question for every man to decide for himself."

SIMON BOLIVAR BUCKNER

Born Kentucky 1823; graduated U.S. Military Academy 1844, eleventh in his class of twenty-five; brevetted 2d lieutenant of infantry, he saw duty on the frontier and taught at West Point; promoted to 2d lieutenant in 1846, he joined General Winfield Scott's command in Mexico, where he was wounded at Churubusco and won brevet promotions to 1st lieutenant and captain; returned briefly to West Point as an instructor in infantry tactics; promoted to 1st lieutenant in 1851 and received the staff rank of captain in 1852; the bulk of his service was on the Western frontier until his resignation from the Army in 1855; Buckner engaged in real estate with his father-in-law in Chicago and managed his wife's substantial holdings; in 1858 settled in Louisville; active in the Kentucky militia, becoming inspector general in 1860; with the coming of the Civil War he worked to secure Kentucky's neutrality, declining a Federal brigadier general's commission proffered by President Abraham Lincoln and General Scott; although Buckner owned no slaves and opposed secession, he opted for the Confederacy following pro-Union posturing in the state legislature; appointed brigadier general in Confederate service in September 1861, he led a force that occupied Bowling Green, Kentucky, shortly thereafter; in February 1862, after senior officers J.B. Floyd and G.J. Pillow fled, Buckner surrendered

Buckner said this was a personal matter and that these circumstances should not influence official action. If he were in command he would surrender the garrison and share its fate, to which Floyd responded, "I place you in command; will you permit me to draw out my brigade?" Buckner replied, "Yes, provided you do so before the enemy act upon my communication."

Floyd then turned to Pillow: "General Pillow, I turn over the

Fort Donelson to his friend and West Point classmate U.S. Grant; imprisoned in Massachusetts until exchanged in August 1862; promoted to major general, he joined the Army of Tennessee; led a division in General Braxton Bragg's Kentucky invasion; given command of the District of the Gulf in December 1862 and the Department of East Tennessee in May 1863; rejoined Bragg's army and led a corps in General James Longstreet's Wing in the victory at Chickamauga; following that battle, Buckner joined a group of officers who called for Bragg's removal and may have penned the petition that many high-ranking generals signed; Bragg retaliated by reducing Buckner to division command and abolishing his Department of East Tennessee; a long illness kept Buckner from active duty until the spring of 1864; he served on the court martial of General Lafayette McLaws and declined the command of General J.B. Hood's former Army of Northern Virginia Division; transferred to the Trans-Mississippi and promoted to lieutenant general in September 1864, Buckner commanded the District of West Louisiana, served as chief of staff for General E. Kirby Smith, and surrendered along with Smith at New Orleans in May 1865; forbidden to leave Louisiana, Buckner worked as a commission merchant and newspaperman until allowed to return to Kentucky in 1868; able to recover his confiscated property in Kentucky and Chicago, he purchased the Louisville *Courier* and served as its editor for twenty years; governor of Kentucky from 1887 to 1892, vice presidential candidate on the "Gold Democrat" ticket in 1896, General Buckner died at his estate near Munfordville in 1914, the last surviving Confederate general above the grade of brigadier. Although he saw limited combat, Buckner performed capably when given the opportunity. His involvement in the anti-Bragg faction no doubt damaged his career.

command." Pillow said instantly, "I pass it." It fell to Buckner, who said, "I assume it; bring on a bugler, pen, ink, and paper." Buckner quickly countermanded an order to destroy commissary supplies at 5:30 in the morning.

An angry Colonel Forrest protested that he had not come to Donelson to surrender and announced his intention to cut his way out even if he saved only one man. He turned to Pillow and asked him what he should do. Pillow replied, "Cut your way out, sir." Forrest then said, "I will do it," and left the room.

At 11:00 PM on the 15th Floyd had telegraphed General Johnston that his forces had won a great victory; Johnston had forwarded the news to Richmond. Four hours later at the conclusion of the conference Floyd telegraphed: "We are completely invested by an army many times our numbers. I regret to say the unanimous opinion of the officers seems to be that we cannot maintain ourselves against these forces."

There were no steamboats at the landing; Floyd had sent them upriver with wounded and prisoners. Pillow, having proclaimed "liberty or death," now chose liberty and escaped by commandeering a flatboat to transport him, his staff, and Gilmer across the Cumberland. They then rode to Clarksville. Two steamers arrived at daybreak, one bringing 400 raw recruits from Nashville. Floyd commandeered the two vessels to rescue his brigade, which consisted of four Virginia regiments and the 20th Mississippi. The steamers ferried two of the Virginia regiments across the river while the 20th Mississippi, given to believe they were to be taken on board with Floyd, stood guard against other increasingly demonstrative Confederate soldiers. Buckner then sent Floyd a message that the vessel would have to depart at once or it would not be allowed to leave. Floyd immediately steamed upriver with his Virginians, leaving the 20th Mississippi, his aide-de-camp, Lieutenant Breckenridge Drake, and the 400 recruits behind. Floyd and Pillow arrived at Nashville on the 17th.

Forrest, meanwhile, announced that he would lead out all

those who wanted to go with him. At 4:00 AM he broke out with his own Tennessee Cavalry Regiment, some artillerymen on their horses, and another 200 troopers from other cavalry commands, perhaps 500 men in all. They reached safety on the river road by fording Lick Creek just south of Dover between the Federal right flank and the river. Forrest recalled that they "crossed a deep slough from the river, saddle-skirt deep." The men encountered no Union troops. Forrest believed the fires spotted by his scouts earlier had been former camp-fires fanned into flame by the wind. He did note that the weather was "intensely cold, a great many of the men were already frost-bitten, and it was the opinion of the generals that the infantry could not have passed through the water and survived it." By the morning of the 18th Forrest and his men were in Nashville. In all perhaps 5,000 Confederates escaped.

Just after daybreak on the 16th the sound of a bugle call from the fort announced an officer with a letter from Buckner to Grant. The Confederate commander requested "the appointment of Commissioners to agree upon terms of capitulation of the forces and fort under my command." He suggested an armistice. Grant was in bed when General Smith came in with the message.

Grant read it and asked Smith what he thought. Smith replied, "I think, no terms with the traitors, by God!" Grant got out of bed, dressed, and drafted the following reply: "Yours of this date, proposing armistice and appointment of Commissions to settle terms of capitulation, is just received. No terms except unconditional and immediate surrender can be accepted. I propose to move immediately upon your works." Smith expressed himself delighted. Buckner replied, "The distribution of the forces under my command, incident to an unexpected change of commanders, and the overwhelming force under your command, compel me, notwithstanding the brilliant success of the Confederate arms yesterday, to accept the ungenerous and unchivalrous terms which you propose."

NATHAN BEDFORD FORREST

Born Tennessee 1821; received little formal education, but by the outbreak of the Civil War he had acquired a substantial fortune as a planter and slave dealer; enlisted as a private in the 7th Tennessee Cavalry, raising and

outfitting at his own expense a battalion of mounted troops that elected him lieutenant colonel in October 1861; during the seige of Fort Donelson, he asked and received permission for his men to break through Union lines and escape surrender; elected colonel of the 3rd Tennessee Cavalry just before Shiloh; in June 1862 assumed command of a cavalry brigade, and the following month captured a Union garrison and its stores at Murfreesboro; promoted to brigadier general, he severed Grant's communications in West Tennessee in December, and in May 1863 saved the railroad between Chattanooga and Atlanta; he participated in the Chattanooga Campaign, but a quarrel with General Bragg caused him to ask for and receive from President Davis an independent command in North Mississippi and West Tennessee; when promoted to major general in December 1863 his fame as a cavalryman had become legendary and "his exploits went unabated till the end of the war"; he captured Fort Pillow in April 1864; in June he brilliantly routed a superior force at Brices Cross Roads; and the following month he checked General A.J. Smith at Tupelo; such lightning blows alarmed General Sherman; Forrest commanded all cavalry under John Bell Hood in the Tennessee Campaign; promoted to lieutenant general in February 1865, Forrest was finally overwhelmed by superior forces at Selma, Alabama, in April 1865. After the war, he returned to planting and was for some years president of the Selma, Marion & Memphis Railroad, which he helped promote. He died, probably of diabetes, at Memphis in 1877, and is buried there. Several military authorities believe he was the greatest cavalry officer produced in America.

As one historian has noted, "Grant had given the Civil War a new, grim, and determined character."

On the morning of February 16 in the dining room of the little Dover Hotel Buckner signed the formal instruments of surrender. Grant was surprised when he arrived to find General Wallace had preceded him by an hour and a half and was then having a cordial breakfast with Buckner and assuring him that Lincoln and Grant were decent folk and that he could expect leniency from them.

Grant ordered all prisoners to be collected under their commanders and issued two days rations before embarking for Cairo. They would be "allowed their clothing, blankets, and such personal property as may be carried about the person, and commissioned officers will be allowed their side arms."

Grant and Buckner had known one another during three years together at West Point and in 1854, when Grant arrived in New York, Buckner had loaned him money. Grant did not forget this and after the surrender he took Buckner aside and offered to reciprocate. In the course of what became a friendly conversation, Buckner noted that had he been in command he would never have allowed Grant to approach Donelson so easily. Grant responded that had Buckner been in command he would never have attempted to invest Donelson with an inferior force while sending an entire brigade around by water. Grant asked what had become of Pillow. "Gone," said Buckner, "he thought you'd rather get hold of him than any other man in the Southern Confederacy." "Oh," Grant cut in, "if I had got him I'd let him go again. He will do us more good commanding you fellows."

Buckner asked permission for Confederate parties to move beyond their lines to bury their dead of the day before, which Grant allowed. Grant recalled that this so accustomed Union soldiers to the comings and goings of the Confederates that some of the latter abused the privilege to escape. One of these was Bushrod Johnson. Not enrolled or reported as a prisoner, he simply walked out through the Federal lines.

Figures on the number of Confederates captured vary. Those given by contemporary Confederate writers range from a high of 17,000 to a low of 11,738. The commissary general of prisoners at Cairo gave 14,623 as the number of men who passed through there on transports from Donelson on their journey to Union prisoner of war camps. Federal troops also secured a considerable quantity of small arms, fifty-seven light and heavy guns, and equipment and rations.

Figures on Confederate killed and wounded vary even more widely than do the numbers on prisoners. General Floyd estimated the number of killed and wounded at 1,500, while Pillow gave 2,000 killed and 1,534 wounded. Union losses were 2,832: 500 killed, 2108 wounded, and 221 captured or missing. McClernand's First Division accounted for half the total: 311 killed, 1,058 wounded and 183 missing or captured. C.F. Smith's Second Division, the next heaviest engaged, lost 145 killed, 819 wounded, and 23 missing or captured; Lew Wallace's Third Division suffered 44 killed, 231 wounded, and 18 missing or captured.

On the 16th Grant telegraphed headquarters of the Department of the Missouri, "I am pleased to announce to you the unconditional surrender this morning of Fort Donelson, with 12,000 to 15,000 prisoners, at least forty pieces of artillery, and a large quantity of stores, horses, mules, and other public property."

6

THE CONSEQUENCES

The capture of Fort Donelson gave the Union its first great victory of the war. It brought elation to the North and sent shock waves through the South. Lincoln well understood its significance. The day of the Confederate surrender, before he knew the outcome, he had written Halleck: "Our success or failure at Donelson is vastly important; and I beg you to put your soul in the effort." After learning of the victory, Secretary of War Edwin M. Stanton wrote Halleck, "The brilliant results of the energetic action in the West fills the Nation with joy." In a hasty note to his wife on the night of the victory, Grant characterized the event as "the largest capture I believe ever made on the continent."

Colonel A.A. Hughes of the 27th Alabama Infantry, who had retreated from Fort Henry only to be surrendered at Donelson, expressed the attitude of the defeated: "a more disgraceful and cowardly surrender never was made by any Generals on Earth than that Made at Donelson on the 16th of Feb 1862 nor a braver or more patriotic set of officers and men never was surrendered in any country."

Strategically, the twin victories of February 1862 gave the Union control of Kentucky and most of middle and western Tennessee. The impact on the Confederacy was immediate and staggering. The Federals had broken the backbone of the Confederacy's defensive line in the West and captured one third of Johnston's already inadequate force in the process. The remaining elements of Johnston's army, dangerously divided by 200 hundred miles, now retreated southward. Johnston had evacuated Bowling Green for Nashville on February 14, but after the fall of Donelson he moved troops south to Murfreesboro. Only days later the Confederates evacuated Columbus. Tennessee and the Deep South lay open to conquest, and the Mississippi was clear down to Island Number Ten. It was Grant's opinion at the time that only the failure of Union leadership, meaning Halleck's refusal to allow a vigorous follow-up, prevented a rapid conquest of the entire Western Theater.

Immediately after the surrender of Donelson, Grant informed Halleck that the path to Clarksville and Nashville was open and that he intended, unless ordered to the contrary, to take Clarksville on the 21st and then move on Nashville. Foote, meanwhile, sent the *Cairo* and six mortar boats up the Cumberland. On the 19th Foote in the *Conestoga* accompanied the *Cairo* upriver. When the vessels came upon Fort Defiance, a small fortification near Clarksville, the crews found a white flag displayed but the fort itself deserted. When General Smith and his men arrived at Clarksville they found it too abandoned.

Late on February 20 Grant and Foote were meeting to plan a joint assault on Nashville, when a telegram arrived from Halleck in which "Old Brains" instructed Foote not to send his gunboats past Clarksville. They were to destroy the bridge and railroad there, after which they were to return to Cairo immediately.

Halleck, evidently concerned by a report that Beauregard was reinforcing Columbus in preparation for an attack against either Paducah or Fort Henry, wanted the gunboats available to defend these places if need be. After learning that the report of Beauregard's activities was false and that Clarksville had been found abandoned, Halleck ordered the gunboats back to Clarksville, but by then Foote and his squadron had already steamed back to Cairo. Foote blamed the failure to seize the moment on Halleck's jealousy of the success achieved by the gunboats in the campaign against Henry and Donelson. Now, back at his base, Foote decided to make sure that his gunboats were completely repaired before resuming offensive operations. Halleck's initial order had indeed been unfortunate. Johnston was still in the process of abandoning Nashville when the gunboats were turned back. Even the appearance of warships might have prevented the Confederates from carrying off a considerable quantity of supplies.

Johnston used the extra time to move what remained of his army out of Grant's reach. His column, which included the Nashville garrison plus the men from Bowling Green and eastern Kentucky, marched south to Murfreesboro before pushing on to Alabama. He planned to make a stand somewhere south of the Tennessee River. For that purpose, the Confederate government rushed reinforcements from across the South. Major General Braxton Bragg's led a large force from Mobile, and other units from Louisiana and eastern Tennessee headed for a concentration point in northern Mississippi. Also, Beauregard and Polk were en route with the Columbus garrison. Ultimately they gathered at Corinth, an important rail center twenty miles inland from the Mississippi River.

No reinforcements from Buell reached Grant until February 24, when General Nelson arrived at Donelson with two brigades. Grant promptly ordered Nelson's Division and a gunboat to Nashville. With Buell also belatedly closing in from the east, on February 25 the Federals took Nashville, which

became the first state capital in the Confederacy to fall to Union troops. But thanks to Forrest's energetic efforts the Confederates got out of the city large quantities of cannon, small arms, ammunition, food, and uniforms, as well as precious foundry equipment.

The way was now clear for Union forces to move down the Mississippi River. The gunboats, fully repaired and their crews brought up to strength at Cairo, kept active patrolling toward Columbus and preventing isolated Confederates from erecting guns along the Cumberland and Tennessee.

Six of Foote's gunboats and eleven mortar boats now worked with Major General John Pope's new Army of the Mississippi to affect the April 8 surrender of strongly fortified Island No. 10 in the Mississippi. Valuable New Orleans fell easily to Admiral David Farragut on April 27. On June 6 the Confederates abandoned Fort Pillow to the Union flotilla. Two days later the key rail link of Memphis on the Mississippi fell.

For a time it appeared that Grant might be prevented from sharing in the fruits of his victory at Donelson. Halleck immediately saw Grant as a rival and tried to claim much of the credit for himself while downplaying Grant's contribution. On February 17 he telegraphed McClellan, "Make Buell, Grant, and Pope major-generals of volunteers, and give me command in the West. I ask this in return for Donelson and Henry." Halleck wanted supreme command in the West, with his rivals Buell and Pope, who had little or nothing at all to do with the victories, under his command. The next day Halleck congratulated General Hunter in Kansas for his alacrity in sending reinforcements to Grant but his only communication to Grant was an order not to let the gunboats go beyond Clarksville.

Indeed, Halleck tried to give credit for the victory at Donelson to General Smith. On February 19 he telegraphed Washington: "Smith, by his coolness and bravery . . . when the battle was against us, turned the tide and carried the enemy's outworks. Make him a major-general. You cannot get a better one. Honor him for this victory, and the whole country will applaud." Halleck's only recognition of Grant's achievement was a formal order, published at St. Louis that same day, in which he thanked Foote, Grant, and their men for the two victories. He made no effort to communicate his thanks to Grant directly.

Upon receiving word of the victory at Fort Donelson and Halleck's recommendation, Lincoln at once sent only Grant's promotion to the Senate, although shortly afterward Buell and Pope also were promoted to major general.

Halleck continued to snipe at a fast-moving Grant who, showing considerable independence, lost contact with his commander. On March 3 Halleck wrote to Washington:

> I have had no communication with General Grant for more than a week. He left his command without my authority and went to Nashville. His army seems to be as much demoralized by the victory at Fort Donelson as that of the Potomac by the defeat at Bull Run. It is hard to censure a successful general immediately after a victory, but I think he richly deserves it. I can get no returns, no reports, no information of any kind from him. Satisfied with his victory, he sits down and enjoys it without any regard for the future. I am worn out and tired with this neglect and inefficiency. C. F. Smith is almost the only officer equal to the emergency.

McClellan responded:

> The future success of our cause demands that proceedings such as Grant's should at once be checked. Generals must observe discipline as well as private soldiers. Do not hesitate to arrest him at once if the good of the service requires it, and place C. F. Smith in command. You are at liberty to regard this as a positive order if it will smooth your way.

Halleck continued to try to undermine Grant. On March 4 he wired McClellan,

> A rumor has just reached me that since the taking of Fort Donelson General Grant has resumed his former bad habits. If so, it will account for his neglect of my often-repeated orders. I do not deem it advisable to arrest him at present, but have placed General Smith in

command of the expedition up the Tennessee. I think
Smith will restore order and discipline.

Halleck then wired Grant, "You will place Major General C.
F. Smith in command of expedition and remain yourself at Fort
Henry. Why do you not obey my orders to report strength and
positions of your command?" In a dignified response on March
5 Grant denied "having disobeyed any order" and said he had
obtained reports on troop strength from all his generals save
Smith. Without bitterness Grant told Halleck that he would
turn over the command of the Tennessee expedition to Smith,
but he pointed out to him that he, Halleck, would be responsible for the troop withdrawals and consequent losses in territory stemming from the transfer of authority. Was he, for example, "to abandon Clarksville entirely or not?" As for Halleck's
order that Grant remain at Fort Henry, that would be difficult
as "The water is about six feet deep inside the fort." The impli-
cation was clear: Halleck was not aware of conditions in his
command area.

On March 5 and 6 Grant set about turning over his command to his old teacher, even graciously congratulating Smith
on his promotion, which he had strongly supported. He also
forwarded his strength figures to Halleck, guessing these
would probably be used, as was indeed the case, to prove that
no major expedition could be undertaken into the South by the
western command without Buell's support—a strong argument
for consolidation under Halleck.

Ironically, Smith, held in such high regard by his contempo-
raries, did not long hold command. After moving the army to
Pittsburg Landing in southwest Tennessee, he jumped into a
small boat, slipped, and badly scraped himself. The wound
became septic and Smith was bedridden. Halleck had no alternative but to restore Grant to command. But for Smith's
untimely injury, Grant's role in the Civil War might have been
dramatically different.

Now back in command of the Army of the Tennessee, Grant prepared to move against the key Confederate rail hub at Corinth, Mississippi. But in a bold strike on April 6 near Pittsburg Landing on the Tennessee, Johnston surprised Grant's army, initiating a bloody contest that came to be known as the Battle of Shiloh. Although away from the army when Johnston struck, Grant rallied his shattered command and managed to hold against repeated Confederate attacks. There is controvery as to how close the South really came to victory at Shiloh. One historian concluded that with 5,000 more men the Confederates would have won decisively, which puts the loss at Fort Donelson in proper perspective. At the height of the fighting on the 6th, Johnston was hit by a musket ball that ruptured a major leg artery. He bled to death before help could reach him. He became the highest ranking American general killed in action in any American war. His sucessor General Beauregard called off the attack at dusk. Grant kept his nerve as his men were driven literally to the banks of the Tennessee. Here, assisted by gunfire from the *Tyler* and *Lexington*, the Federals held. The arrival of 21,000 fresh troops under Buell that night allowed Grant to turn the battle the next day. But the near disaster again placed Grant's career in jeopardy.

The Confederates retreated to Corinth. General Halleck soon arrived to take personal command of the march on the Corinth. Entrenching every mile, the cautious Halleck took more than a month to move his army some twenty miles. By the time the Federals reached the rail hub in late May, the Confederates had moved on. The conquest of the South had only just begun.

The Federal victories at Forts Henry and Donelson had an important impact on the prosecution of the war in the West and on many careers on both sides of the conflict. Following the surrender of Donelson, Generals Floyd and Pillow were relieved from duty pending an investigation into their conduct.

Although charges against them were later dismissed, neither officer again held a prominent command. Floyd subsequently took a position with the Virginia Home Guard but his health soon broke and he died in 1863. Although he was found guilty of "grave errors in judgment in the military operations which resulted in the surrender of the army," Pillow was returned to duty in August. He spent most of the rest of the war in various administrative assignments. After the war he practiced law. General Bushrod Johnson was badly wounded at Shiloh but recovered and participated in a number of battles, including Murfreesboro (Stones River) and Chickamauga. He became a major general in May 1864 and after the war was chancellor of the University of Nashville.

Simon Bolivar Buckner and the remaining Confederate prisoners of war were exchanged in the fall of 1862. Promoted to major general and then to lieutenant general, Buckner fought in many of the later Western battles. He had the grim distinction of surrendering the Trans-Mississippi Department to Federal authorities in May 1865. After the war he edited the Louisville *Courier* and from 1887 to 1892 was governor of Kentucky. His friendship with Grant survived the war, and he served as a pallbearer at Grant's funeral in 1885. The last surviving Confederate lieutenant general, Buckner died in 1914.

Lloyd Tilghman was also exchanged in the fall of 1862 but unlike Buckner did not survive the war. He was killed during the Vicksburg Campaign in the Battle of Champion Hill, May 16, 1863.

Nathan Bedford Forrest, a wealthy self-made man with no military experience when the war broke out, rose to the rank of lieutenant general and became one of the Confederacy's most brilliant and innovative cavalry commanders. Later he was Grand Wizard of the first Ku Klux Klan, which he ordered disbanded at the end of Reconstruction.

General Johnston, thought by many Southerners at the time to be the Confederacy's ablest general, saw that reputation greatly tarnished by the losses of Henry and Donelson. These defeats and the need to turn back the Federal invasion of the South led to his bold and desperate attack at Shiloh, where he appeared to be on the verge of a great victory when struck down on the first bloody day of that battle. Historian T. Harry Williams has noted that he was "like the promising artist who dies young. The critics exclaim that if his life had been spared he would have done something great. The trouble is, no one can ever tell. Nothing that Johnston did in his brief career justifies the belief that he had the elements of greatness. Many things that he did suggest that he was not qualified for high command."

Oddly, the triumphs of February 1862 marked the career pinnacle for many of the leading participants. Grant won quick promotion to major general and by March all three of Grant's divisional commanders were advanced to the same grade. At the same time, the colonels commanding brigades were made brigadier generals. The Union naval commanders were only recognized in July after other victories, when the gunboat commanders were advanced one grade in rank and Foote was promoted to rear admiral.

Although wounded in the attack on Fort Donelson, Foote refused to be slowed and participated on crutches in the successful attack on Island No. 10. But the wound exacted a toll and in May 1862 he took leave from the Mississippi Squadron. Foote expected soon to return to his post but he never completely regained his health. He died in June 1863.

C.F. Smith, who had performed so well during the Tennessee Campaign, never recovered from the freak wound that cost him his army command. Moved to Grant's headquarters at Savannah, Tennessee, to recuperate, he died there on April 25, 1862.

The ambitious and pompous McClernand toyed with the idea of unseating Grant as primary commander in the West. He directed a corps through most of the 1863 Vicksburg

Campaign until Grant relieved him. He briefly held a corps command in the 1864 Red River Campaign but fared so poorly that he resigned his commission and returned to Illinois politics.

Lew Wallace commanded a division at Shiloh but his performance on the first day of that battle drew Grant's criticism and he was relieved. In 1864 at Monocacy Junction, Maryland, he commanded a patchwork force that attempted to block Confederate General Jubal Early's drive on Washington. Although driven from the field, Wallace's command bought valuable time to ready the capital's defense. After the war Wallace participated in the trial of the Lincoln assassination conspirators. He was subsequently governor of New Mexico Territory and also minister to Turkey. A facile writer, Wallace achieved lasting fame for his novel *Ben Hur: A Tale of the Christ*, published in 1880.

On March 11 Halleck received his reward, being named to command the huge new Department of the Mississippi, which included the former Departments of the Missouri, the Ohio, and Kansas. But Halleck's one foray as a field commander, the advance on Corinth in May 1862, showed his excessively cautious tendencies. Named general-in-chief of the Union Army in July 1862, Halleck displayed considerable administrative talents but made many enemies over his failure to grasp the realities in the field. In March 1864, when Grant became supreme commander of all Union armies, Halleck was shifted to the new position of chief of staff, in which he remained until the end of the war and rendered valuable service.

Unlike most of the leading participants in the events of February 1862, Grant enjoyed remarkable success, becoming the single most important military figure of the Civil War. The victories at Forts Henry and Donelson brought U. S. ("Unconditional Surrender") Grant lasting fame. One account of the events at Fort Donelson, published in the Northern press, depicted Grant chewing on a cigar throughout the battle. Grateful Northerners promptly sent him more than 5,000 cigars.

Grant's dignified and careful responses to Halleck's attacks were heeded in Washington. Nine of his senior officers, including McClernand, rallied to him, signing a letter to Grant deploring his removal from command. Although Halleck enjoyed McClellan's support, Grant had more powerful support in the White House and War Department. Lincoln himself ordered Halleck either to bring charges against Grant or end the campaign to smear him. When Halleck received overall command of forces in the West he no longer had to fear him, and in late March he restored Grant to command.

But the near catastrophe on the first day of Shiloh and ghastly bloodshed of that battle (nearly 24,000 casualties on the two sides) brought calls for his dismissal and renewed allegations of drunkenness. Lincoln, pressed by Grant's critics to fire him, replied, "I cannot spare this man; he fights." Grant rewarded the president's confidence in him with major victories at Vicksburg and Chattanooga in 1863. In March 1864 Lincoln elevated Grant to the post of general-in-chief of the Armies of the United States, complete with the three-star rank of lieutenant general, making him the first U.S. Army officer since George Washington to be confirmed at that grade. Grant then moved east to direct the effort against General Robert E. Lee. After a bloody eleven-month campaign across Virginia, the improbable story that began with one surrender ended with another, when Grant met the once-invincible Lee at Appomattox Court House on April 9, 1865.

APPENDIX A

ORGANIZATION OF UNION FORCES AT FORT DONELSON, FEBRUARY12-16, 1862

DISTRICT OF CAIRO
BRIG. GEN. ULYESSES S. GRANT

FIRST DIVISION
BRIG. GEN. JOHN A. McCLERNAND

FIRST BRIGADE
COL. RICHARD J. OGLESBY
8th Illinois
18th Illinois
29th Illinois
30th Illinois
31st Illinois
Illinois Light Artillery, Battery A
2d Illinois Light Artillery, Battery E
2d Illinois Cavalry, Companies A and B
2d U.S. Cavalry, Company C
4th U.S. Cavalry, Company I
Carmichael's Illinois Cavalry
Dollins' Illinois Cavalry
O'Harnett's Illinois Cavalry
Stewart's Illinois Cavalry

SECOND BRIGADE
COL. WILLIAM H. L. WALLACE
11th Illinois
20th Illinois
45th Illinois
48th Illinois
1st Illinois Light Artillery, Battery B
1st Illinois Light Artillery, Battery D
4th Illinois Cavalry

THIRD BRIGADE
COL. WILLIAM R. MORRISON (WOUNDED)
COL. LEONARD F. ROSS
17th Illinois
49th Illinois

SECOND DIVISION
BRIG. GEN. CHARLES F. SMITH

FIRST BRIGADE
COL. JOHN McARTHUR
9th Illinois
12th Illinois
41st Illinois

THIRD BRIGADE
COL. JOHN COOK
7th Illinois
50th Illinois
52d Illinois
14th Iowa
13th Missouri
1st Missouri Light Artillery, Battery D
1st Missouri Light Artillery, Battery H
1st Missouri Light Artillery, Battery K

FOURTH BRIGADE
COL. JACOB G. LAUMAN
25th Indiana
2d Iowa
7th Iowa
14th Iowa
Birge's Sharpshooters

FIFTH BRIGADE
COL. MORGAN L. SMITH
8th Missouri
11th Indiana

THIRD DIVISION
BRIG. GEN. LEWIS WALLACE

FIRST BRIGADE
COL. CHARLES CRUFT
31st Indiana
44th Indiana
17th Kentucky
25th Kentucky

SECOND BRIGADE
(attached to Third Brigade)
46th Illinois
57th Illinois
58th Illinois

THIRD BRIGADE
COL. JOHN M. THAYER
1st Nebraska
58th Ohio
68th Ohio
76th Ohio

NOT BRIGADED
1st Illinois Light Artillery, Battery A
32d Illinois, Company A

APPENDIX B

ORGANIZATION OF CONFEDERATE FORCES AT FORT DONELSON, FEBRUARY 12-16, 1862

POST COMMANDER
BRIG. GEN. JOHN B. FLOYD
BRIG. GEN. GIDEON PILLOW (February 12)
BRIG. GEN. SIMON B. BUCKNER (February 16)

BUCKNER'S DIVISION (RIGHT WING)

BRIG. GEN. SIMON B. BUCKNER

SECOND BRIGADE
(Three regiments temporarily attached to Third Brigade)
2d Kentucky
14th Mississippi
41st Tennessee

THIRD BRIGADE
COL. JOHN C. BROWN
3d Tennessee
18th Tennessee
32d Tennessee

ARTILLERY
Graves' Kentucky Battery
Porter's Tennessee Battery

PILLOW'S DIVISION (LEFT WING)

BRIG. GEN. GIDEON PILLOW
BRIG. GEN. BUSHROD JOHNSON

HEIMAN'S BRIGADE
COL. A. HEIMAN
27th Alabama
10th Tennessee
42d Tennessee

48th Tennessee
53d Tennessee
MANEY'S TENNESSEE BATTERY

DAVIDSON'S BRIGADE
COL. T. J. DAVIDSON
COL. J. M. SIMONTON
8th Kentucky
1st Mississippi
3d Mississippi
7th Texas

DRAKE'S BRIGADE
COL. JOSEPH DRAKE
Alabama Battalion
15th Arkansas
4th Mississippi
Tennessee Battalion

WHARTON'S BRIGADE (FLOYD'S DIVISION)
COL. G. C. WHARTON
51st Virginia
56th Virginia

MCCAUSLAND'S BRIGADE (FLOYD'S DIVISION)
COL. JOHN McCAUSLAND
36th Virginia
50th Virginia

BALDWIN'S BRIGADE (FROM BUCKNER'S DIVISION)
COL. WILLIAM E. BALDWIN
20th Mississippi (temporarily from McCausland's Brigade)
26th Mississippi
26th Tennessee

ARTILLERY
Green's Kentucky Battery
French's Virginia Battery
Guy's Virginia Battery

GARRISON
COL. JOHN W. HEAD
30th Tennessee

49th Tennessee
50th Tennessee

FORT BATTERIES
CAPT. JOSEPH DIXON (KILLED)
CAPT. JACOB CULBERSON
Company A, 30th Tennesse Infantry
Company A, 50th Tennessee Infantry
Ross's (Maury) Tennessee Battery

CAVALRY
COL. NATHAN B. FORREST
Forrest's Tennessee Regiment
Tennessee Battalion

ABOUT THE BIOGRAPHICAL SKETCHES

The biographical sketches that accompany the photographs in this volume were derived from numerous sources and written by David Coffey and Grady McWhiney.

SELECTED BIBLIOGRAPHY

Ambrose, Stephen E. *The Campaigns for Fort Donelson: A Review.* Conshohocken, PA: Eastern Acorn Press, 1983.

Bearss, Edwin C. *Unconditional Surrender: The Fall of Fort Donelson.* Dover, TN: Eastern National Park and Monument Association, 1962.

The Campaigns of Fort Donelson: A Review of the Encounter with Vignettes of the Men Who Fought and Articles on the Surrounding Action. Conshohocken, PA: Eastern Acorn Press, 1992.

Coombe, Jack D. *Thunder Along the Mississippi: The River Battles that Split the Confederacy.* New York: Sarpedon, 1996.

Cooling, B. Franklin. *Fort Donelson's Legacy: War and Society in Kentucky and Tennessee, 1862–1863.* Knoxville, TN: University of Tennessee Press, 1996.

_____. *Forts Henry and Donelson: The Key to the Confederate Heartland.* Knoxville, TN: University of Tennessee Press, 1987.

Connelly, Thomas L. *Army of the Heartland: The Army of Tennessee, 1861–1862.* Baton Rouge: Louisiana State University Press, 1967.

Daniel, Larry J. *Island No. 10: Struggle for the Mississippi Valley.* Tuscaloosa, AL: University of Alabama Press, 1996.

Force, M. F. *From Fort Henry to Corinth.* Reprint. Wilmington, NC: Broadfoot Publishing Co., 1989. (Reprint of 1881.)

Fox, Gustavus. *Confidential Correspondence of Gustavus Vasa Fox, Assistant Secretary of the Navy, 1861–1865*. Edited by Robert Means Thompson and Richard Wainwright. New York: De Vinne Press, 1918.

Gosnell, Harper Allen. *Guns on the Western Waters*. Baton Rouge: Lousiana State University Press, 1949.

Grant, Ulysses S. *Memoirs and Selected Letters*. New York: Library of America, 1990.

Hamilton, James J. *The Battle of Fort Donelson*. New York: Thomas Yoseloff, 1968.

Hattaway, Herman, and Archer Jones. *How the North Won: A Military History of the Civil War*. Urbana, IL: University of Illinois Press, 1983.

Headley, J. T. *Farragut and Our Naval Commanders*. New York: E.B. Treat, 1867.

Hoppin, James M. *The Life of Andrew Hull Foote, Rear Admiral, United States Navy*. New York: Harper & Brothers, 1874.

Hughes, Cheairs Nathaniel, Jr. and Roy P. Stonesifer, Jr. *The Life & Wars of Gideon J. Plllow*. Chapel Hill, NC: The University of North Carolina Press, 1993.

Johnson, R. U. and C. C. Buel, Editors. *Battles and Leaders of the Civil War*. 4 vols. Reprint. Secaucus, NJ: Castle, nd.

Keller, Allan. *Andrew Hull Foote: Gunboat Commodore (1806–1863)*.
Hartford: Connecticut Civil War Centennial Commission, 1969.

King, George L. *Campaign of Fort Henry and Donelson, 1862*. Fort Benning, GA: Infantry Series, 1928.

Macartney, Clarence Edward. *Mr. Lincoln's Admirals*. New York: Funk & Wagnalls, 1956.

McFeely, William S. *Grant, A Biography*. New York: W.W. Norton, 1981.

Milligan, John D. *Gunboats Down the Mississippi*. Annapolis, MD: Naval Institute Press, 1965.

Nevin, David and the editors of Time-Life Books. *The Civil War: The Road to Shiloh and the Early Battles in the West.* Alexandria, VA: Time-Life Boooks, 1983.

Page, Dave. *Ships Versus Shore: Civil War Engagements along Southern Shores and Rivers.* Nashille, TN: Rutledge Hill Press, 1994.

Porter, Admiral David D. *Naval History of the Civil War.* Reprint. Secaucus, NJ: Castle Books, 1984.

Reed, Rowena. *Combined Operations in the Civil War.* Annapolis, MD: Naval Institute Press, 1978.

Roland, Charles P. *Albert Sidney Johnston: Soldier of Three Republics.* Austin, TX: University of Texas Press, 1964.

_____. *Jefferson Davis's Greatest General: Albert Sidney Johnston.* Abilene, TX: McWhiney Foundation Press, 2000.

Silverstone, Paul H. *Warships of the Civil War Navies.* Annapolis, MD: Naval Institute Press, 1989.

Stern, Philip Van Doren. *The Confederate Navy: A Pictorial History.* Garden City, New York: Doubleday & Co., 1962.

The Campaigns for Fort Donelson: A Review of the Encounter with Vignettes of the Men Who Fought and Articles on the Surrounding Action. NP: Eastern Acorn Press, 1983.

Tucker, Spencer C. *Andrew Foote: Civil War Admiral on Western Waters.* Annapolis, MD: Naval Institute Press, 2000.

U.S. Navy Department, Naval History Division. *Riverine Warfare: The U.S. Navy's Operations on Inland Waters.* Revised edition. Washington: Government Printing Office, 1969.

U.S. Navy Department. *Offical Records of the Union and Confederate Navies in the War of the Rebellion.* Series 1, Volume 22. Washington: Government Printing Office, 1908.

U.S. War Department. *The War of the Rebellion. A Compilation of the Official Records of the Union and Confederate Armies.* 128 vols. Washington: Government Printing Office, 1882, 1880–1901.

Walke, Henry. *Naval Scenes and Reminiscences of the Civil War in the United States.* New York: F. R. Reed, 1877.

Welles, Gideon. *Diary of Gideon Welles, Secretary of the Navy Under Lincoln and Johnson.* Edited by Howard K. Beale and Alan W. Brownsword. Boston: H. Mifflin Co., 1911.

Williams, Kenneth P. *Lincoln Finds a General.* 5 volumes. New York: MacMillan, 1949–1959.

Winschel, Terrence J. *Vicksburg: Fall of the Confederate Gibraltar.* Abilene, TX: McWhiney Foundation Press, 1999

Articles

Ambrose, Stephen E. "The Union Command System and the Donelson Campaign," *Military Affairs* (Spring 1960).

Bearss, Edwin C. "The Fall of Fort Henry, Tennesse," *West Tennesse Historical Society Journal* (1963).

_____. "Unconditional Surrender: The Fall of Fort Donelson," *Tennessee Historical Quarterly* (March–June 1962).

Milligan, John D. "Andrew Foote: Zealous Reformer, Administrator, Warrior," *Captains of the Old Steam Navy. Makers of the American Naval Tradition, 1840–1880.* Edited by James C. Bradford. Annapolis, Maryland: Naval Institute Press, 1986.

PHOTO CREDITS

We gratefully acknowledge the Library of Congress for the photos of Simon Bolivar Buckner, Don Carlos Buell, John B. Floyd, Andrew Hull Foote, Ulysses S. Grant, John A. McClernand, Gideon J. Pillow, Lew Wallace, and the Federal gunboat *St. Louis.*

We appreciate the assistance of the United States Army Military History Institute at Carlisle Barracks, Pennsylvania, in providing the photos of Nathan Bedford Forrest, Henry Halleck, and Leonidas Polk.

We thank the National Archives for the photos of Albert Sidney Johnston and Charles F. Smith.

The photo of Lloyd Tilghman is from *Generals in Gray: Lives of the Confederate Commanders* by Ezra J. Warner (Baton Rouge: Louisiana State University Press, 1959).

The photo of the Conestoga is courtesy of the Public Library of Cincinnati and Hamilton County.

The illustration of the Columbiad on a barbette carriage is from the United States War Department, *Atlas to Accompany the Official Records of the Union and Confederate Armies* (Washington, DC: Government Printing Office, 1891–1895).

The photo of the Upper Water Battery at Fort Donelson is courtesy of Donald S. Frazier, Ph.D., Abilene, Texas.

INDEX